1 Foreword

This Exam Preparation book is intended for those preparing for the Open Group Architecture Framework Certification.

The Art of Service has been an Accredited Training Organization for this program since 1998. The strategies and content in this book are a result of experience and understanding of the TOGAF distinctions, and the exam requirements.

This book is **not** a replacement for completing the course. This is a study aid to assist those who have completed an accredited course and preparing for the exam.

Do not underestimate the value of your own notes and study aids. The more you have, the more prepared you will be.

While it is not possible to pre-empt every question and content that MAY be asked in the exam, this book covers the main concepts covered within The Open Group Architecture Framework discipline.

The advantages of using the TOGAF approach are that it provides:

- A process for designing an information system, in terms of a set of building blocks.
- Establishes a common vocabulary for use in the design, implementation and governance.
- Includes a list of recommended standards to use with the organization's enterprise architecture.
- Contains a set of structured and rigorous methods for the implementation and governance of enterprise architecture.

Due to licensing rights, we are unable to provide actual TOGAF Exams. However, the study notes and sample exam questions in this book will allow you to more easily prepare for a TOGAF exam.

Ivanka Menken
Executive Director
The Art of Service

Copyright The Art of Service | Brisbane, Australia | Email:service@theartofservice.com
Web: http://theartofservice.com | eLearning: http://theartofservice.org | Phone: +61 (0)7 3252 2055

Write a review to receive any *free* eBook from our Catalogue - $99 Value!

If you recently bought this book, we would love to hear from you! Benefit from receiving a free eBook from our catalogue at http://www.emereo.org/ if you write a review on Amazon (or the online store where you purchased this book) about your last purchase!

How does it work?

To post a review on Amazon, just log in to your account and click on the Create your own review button (under Customer Reviews) of the relevant product page. You can find examples of product reviews in Amazon. If you purchased from another online store, simply follow their procedures.

What happens when I submit my review?

Once you have submitted your review, send us an email at review@emereo.org with the link to your review, and the eBook you would like as our thank you from http://www.emereo.org/. Pick any book you like from the catalogue, up to $99 RRP. You will receive an email with your eBook as download link. It is that simple!

2 Table of Contents

4

6

Copyright The Art of Service | Brisbane, Australia | Email:service@theartofservice.com
Web: http://theartofservice.com | eLearning: http://theartofservice.org | Phone: +61 (0)7 3252 2055

3   The Open Group Architecture Framework

The Open Group is a consortium neutral to vendor and technology and intent on creating open standards and global interoperability to enable access to integrated information within and between enterprises. The Open Group Architecture Forum (TOGAF) provides an opportunity for service providers and tool vendors to demonstrate their products and services ability to support the enterprise. TOGAF is an industry standard architecture framework to develop information systems architecture within the enterprise using the TOGAF Architecture Development Method (ADM).

Certification for TOGAF comes in two levels or parts:
- Foundation
- Certified.

Foundation Certification demonstrates a candidate's knowledge of the terminology, and basic concepts of TOGAF, as well as the core principles. The Certified level shows a candidate's ability to apply their knowledge of TOGAF.

The TOGAF 9 Part 1 exam covers the following eleven topics:
1. Basic Concepts
2. Core Concepts
3. Introduction to the ADM
4. The Enterprise Continuum and Tools
5. ADM Phases
6. ADM Guidelines and Techniques
7. Architecture Governance
8. Architecture Views, Viewpoints and Stakeholders
9. Building Blocks
10. ADM Deliverables
11. TOGAF Reference Models

The TOGAF 9 Part 2 exam draws its questions from the following topic areas:

- ADM Phases: Project Establishment
- ADM Phases: Architecture Definition
- ADM Phases: Transition Planning
- ADM Phases: Governance
- Adapting the ADM
- Architecture Content Framework
- TOGAF Reference Models
- Architecture Capability Framework

4   Exam Specifics

TOGAF 9 Part 1 – Foundation exam is a comprised of 40 simple multiple choice questions to be completed in one hour. A candidate must pass the exam with 55% of the questions answered correctly. There are no prerequisites to take this exam.

TOGAF 9 Part 2 – Certified exam is comprised of eight complex scenario questions with gradient scoring to be completed in 90 minutes. A candidate must pass with a score of 60 or better. In order to take the exam, the candidate must be certified to TOGAF 9 Foundation or take and pass the Part 1 exam on the same day from the same test provider providing the Part 2 exam. This test is open book.

The Open Group exams are proctored by Prometric Services. Scheduling and location of test sites can be obtained at www.prometric.com. Tests are conducted at a testing center. Two valid forms of ID are required when arriving at the center. Training in TOGAF is required and a voucher for completing training, self-study or classroom, is required.

If a candidate fails an exam, they must wait at least one month before retaking.

5 The Open Group Architecture Framework

5.1 TOGAF Overview

The Open Group Architecture Framework (TOGAF) provides several opportunities for enterprise architects and IT organizations, including:
- an iterative process model supported by best practices
- A re-usable set of existing architecture assets
- Methods and tools for the acceptance, development, use, and maintenance of an enterprise architecture

5.1.1 Defining Architecture

The definition of 'architecture' from ISO/IEC 42010:2007 is:
> "The fundamental organization of a system, embodied in its components, their relationships to each other and the environment, and the principles governing its design and evolution."

TOGAF supports this definition by remaining consistent with the terminology of the ISO/IEC 42010:2007 but views the meaning of 'architecture' differently based on the context used. For TOGAF, architectures are:
- A formal description of a system, or detailed plan of a system at the component level for guiding implementation.
- The structure of components, their relationships to each other, and the principles and guidelines underlining there design and evolution over time.

An enterprise architecture is comprised of four commonly accepted domains:
- Business Architecture
- Data Architecture
- Applications Architecture
- Technology Architecture

5.1.2   Approaches to Architecture Development

On large scale, complex architecture development projects, the focus and scope of the project is a critical component to the project's success. Two approaches are typically adopted:
- Vertical Approach – enterprise is divided into segments representing independent business sector.
- Horizontal Approach – enterprise is divided into architecture domains.

5.1.3   Architecture Capability

Creating architecture for an enterprise requires that the organization have the business capability to support the architecture through structures, roles, responsibilities, skills, and processes.

TOGAF architecture capability builds on the Architecture Repository and Enterprise Continuum by identifying the architecture components providing the capability and their relationships to each other. The components include:
- Skilled Resource Pool
- Roles and Responsibilities
- Contracts
- Projects and Portfolios
- Governance of Projects and Portfolios
- Business Operations
- Governance Bodies

Enterprise Architectures look to establish capabilities in the areas of:
- Financial Management
- Performance Management
- Service Management
- Risk Management
- Communications and Stakeholder Management
- Quality Management
- Supplier Management
- Configuration Management
- Environment Management

5.2.1   Architecture Development Method

The Architecture Development Method (ADM) is the core component of TOGAF, providing a tested and repeatable process for developing architectures.

The phases of the ADM include:
- Preliminary – Prepares the organization.
- Architecture Vision – sets the scope, constraints, and expectations.
- Business Architecture – develops baseline and target architectures for Business Architecture.
- Information Systems Architecture – develops baseline and target architectures for Information Systems Architecture.
- Technology Architecture – develops baseline and target architectures for Technology Architecture.
- Opportunities and Solutions – performs initial implementation planning.
- Migration Planning – analyses costs, benefits, and risks.
- Implementation Governance – provides architectural oversight to implementation.
- Architecture Change Management – provides continual monitoring and a change management process.
- Requirements Management – validates and enforces business requirements.

5.2.2   Architecture Content Framework

The output of the ADM comes in many forms. To ensure consistency, the Architecture Content Framework defines the type of architectural work product found, such as:
- Deliverable – a formally agreed upon work product of the project output.
- Artifact – An architectural work product describing the architecture from a specific viewpoint.

- Building Block – A component of business, IT or architecture capability combined with other building blocks to create architectures and solutions. Building blocks typically include:
  - Architecture Building Blocks (ABB)
  - Solution Building Blocks (SBB)

5.2.3   Enterprise Continuum

Architecture and solution artifacts are collected into an Architecture Repository. The Enterprise Continuum is a comprehensive view of this repository and is comprised of two concepts:
- Architecture Continuum
- Solutions Continuum

The Architecture Repository stores architecture output at different levels of abstraction created by the ADM.   In conjunction with the Enterprise Continuum, stakeholders and providers have the means to understand and cooperated within the architecture.

5.2.4   Architecture Repository

The primary components of the Architecture Repository include:
- Architecture Metamodel: the application of an architecture framework for a specific enterprise
- Architecture Capability – the parameters, structures, and processes supporting the governance of the Architecture
- Architecture Landscape – the architecture view of building blocks currently in use within the enterprise
- Standards Information Base (SIB) – the standards requiring compliance for architectures
- Reference Library – provides the guidelines, templates, patterns, and reference materials to leverage during the creation of the enterprise
- Governance Log – a record of governance activity across the enterprise

5.2.5   Architecture Patterns

A pattern is a reusable object that was useful in one practical situation and has the potential to be useful in other similar situations. Formalizing the process to capture patterns is beneficial for an organization as a way to acknowledge, build, and share best practices in support.

The content of a pattern contains:
- Name – unique heading reference for the pattern
- Problem – description of the situation where pattern is applied
- Context – the existing preconditions where the pattern is applicable
- Forces – description of the relevant forces and constraints
- Solution – description of pattern details
- Resulting Context – the post-conditions present after applying the pattern
- Examples – sample applications of the pattern
- Rationale – a explanation of the pattern
- Related Problems – a description of any relationships between this pattern and other patterns
- Known Uses – known applications of the pattern in the existing systems

5.2.6   Architecture Principles

Principles are general rules and guidelines intended to inform and support the organization's fulfillment of its mission.

Principles can be established on any or all levels of the organization:
- Enterprise – provides a basis for decision-making throughout the enterprise
- Information Technology – provides guidance on the use and development of all IT resources and assets
- Architecture – IT principles that relate to architecture work

Criteria have been identified to distinguish a good set of principles:

- Understandable
- Robust
- Complete
- Consistent
- Stable

Documentation format of a principle includes:

- Name
- Statement
- Rationale
- Implication

Below is an example list of principles from the US Government's Federal Enterprise Architecture Framework (FEAF):

- Business Principles
  - Primacy of Principles
  - Maximum Benefit to the Enterprise
  - Information Management is Everybody's Business
  - Business Continuity
  - Common Use Applications
  - Service Orientation
  - Compliance with Law
  - IT Responsibility
  - Protection of Intellectual Property
- Data Principles
  - Data is an Asset
  - Data is Shared
  - Data is Accessible
  - Data Trustee
  - Common Vocabulary and Data Definition
  - Data Security
- Application Principles
  - Technology Independence
  - Ease-of-Use
- Technology Principles
  - Requirements-Based Change
  - Responsive Change Management
  - Control Technical Diversity
  - Interoperability

5.2.7   Architecture Skills Framework

Skill frameworks provide a perspective on competency levels required for roles and define:
- The roles within a work area
- The skills required for each role
- The knowledge required to successfully fulfill a role

Skills are identified by the category they fall into:
- Generic Skills
- Business Skills and Methods
- Enterprise Architecture Skills
- Program or Project Management Skills
- IT General Knowledge Skills
- Technical IT Skills
- Legal Environment

Skills a re further categorized by applying four levels of knowledge or proficiency, which are:
- Background – no required skill but can be managed and defined
- Assurance – understands the background and advise client accordingly
- Knowledge – detailed knowledge of subject area
- Expert – extensive and substantial practical experience

5.2.8   Architecture Capability Framework

The Architecture Capability Framework is based on the Capability Maturity Models (CMM), which provides an effective method for enabling an organization to gain control and improve its IT-related development processes in a gradual manner.

Several models are available for use:
- Capability Maturity Model Integration (CMMI)
- Software Acquisition Capability Maturity Model (SA-CMM)
- Systems Engineering Capability Maturity Model (SE-CMM)
- People Capability Maturity Model (P-CMM)
- IDEAL Life Cycle Model for Improvement

19

- IT Architecture Capabilities Maturity Model (ACMM)

The ACMM is comprised of three sections:
- The IT architecture maturity model
- IT architecture characteristics of processes at different maturity levels
- The ACMM scorecard

Six levels of maturity are present for nine architecture characteristics:
- The Levels
    - 0   None
    - 1   Initial
    - 2   Under Development
    - 3   Defined
    - 4   Managed
    - 5   Measured
- The Characteristics
    - IT architecture process
    - IT architecture development
    - Business linkage
    - Senior management involvement
    - Operating unit participation
    - Architecture communication
    - IT security
    - Architecture governance
    - IT investment and acquisition strategy

6 Architecture Development Method

6.1 Using the Architecture Development Method

The Architecture Development Method (ADM) provides a formal approach to developing the architectural components required to meet the business needs of an enterprise.

The Enterprise Continuum is a framework for supporting the leveraged use of relevant architecture assets while executing the ADM. It provides a way to categorize architecture reference material, both from an organization's Architecture Repository and the industry's relevant reference models.

6.1.1 Architecture Repository

The Architecture Repository is a set of reference architectures, models, and patterns acceptable for use within an enterprise, as well as the actual architectural work performed in the environment previously. The repository is populated as the ADM is executed.

Architecture development is a continuous, cyclical process. Though the ADM is primarily focused on the development of an enterprise-specific architecture, it is also a method of populating the Architecture Repository.

6.1.2 Foundation Architecture

The Foundation Architecture consists of re-usable common models, policies, and governance definitions. At the beginning of an organization's attempt to design their enterprise, the definitions and selections in the Foundation Architecture are undeveloped and scarce.

The ADM provides support in identifying and developing the content of the Foundation Architecture to be used to define more detailed architectures for the enterprise.

6.1.3 Guidelines and Techniques

The application of the ADM is supported by the use of a set of resources such as:
- Architecture Principles
- Stakeholder Management
- Architecture Patterns
- Business Scenarios
- Gap Analysis
- Migration Planning Techniques
- Interoperability Requirements
- Business Transformation Readiness Assessment
- Risk Management
- Capability-Based Planning

6.1.4 Development Cycle

Some key points applicable to the Architecture Development Method include:
- The development cycle is iterative across the whole process, between and within phases. Each iteration of the ADM requires decisions in:
  - the coverage of the enterprise involved
  - the level of detailed required
  - the time period for developments
  - the architectural assets being leveraged
- A practical assessment of resource availability and competence should exist for each iteration.
- The ADM is intended for use in different geographies, vertical sectors and industries of the enterprise.

6.1.5 ADM Structure

The structure of the ADM is through phases:
- Preliminary
- A. Architecture Vision
- B. Business Architecture
- C. Information Systems Architectures
- D. Technology Architectures
- E. Opportunities and Solutions
- F. Migration Planning
- G. Implementation Governance
- H. Architecture change Management
- Requirements Management

Each phase consists of specific steps to be completed to consistently met the objectives of the effort.

6.1.6 Architecture Governance

Architecture Governance aligns the framework with current best practices and ensures an appropriate level of visibility, guidance and control to support the stakeholder's requirements and obligations.

A controlled environment should manage architectural artifacts, governance, and related processes. The major information areas related to architecture governance to be managed are:
- Reference Data – provides guidance and instruction during project implementation.
- Process Status – manages the governance processes and information acquired by the process.
- Audit Information – recorded process actions to support key decisions and responsible personnel, and provide a reference for future process develop0ments, guidance, and precedence.

6.1.7   Architecture Integration

Integrating individual architectures provide the foundation for interoperability, migration, and conformance between those architectures. Referred to as a meta-architecture framework, its purpose is to:

- Provide a basis for understanding how components fit into the overall framework
- Enable architectural models to be created that focus on enterprise-level capabilities
- Define the conformance standards to enable maximum leverage and re-use of architecture components

6.2   Architecture Scope

Scope of the architecture is typically determined by:

- The availability of people, finance, and other resources
- The objectives and stakeholder concerns addressed in the architecture
- The organizational authority of the architecture team

The four dimensions used to define and limit the scope include:

- Enterprise Scope or Focus
- Architecture Domains
- Vertical Scope
- Time Period

6.2.1   Enterprise Scope or Focus

Specifically in large-scale architecture developments, the use of federated architectures is found: independently developed, maintained, and managed architectures by specific business units and integrated into a meta-architecture framework. Federated architecture development is usually vertical or horizontal.

Vertical development focuses on separating the enterprise into segments representing an independent business function within the enterprise. Each function has its own architecture potentially

24

including all four domains. Integration with the rest of the enterprise is secondary to the function's own environment.

Horizontal development concentrates on the creation of architectural "super-domains" where each architecture domain covers the entire enterprise.

6.2.2   Architecture Domains

All four architecture domains are addressed in complete enterprise architecture; but constraints on time, funding, or resources typically restrict the level of focus available to an architecture project. Typically, projects are determined by specific business drivers. Still, risks and other considerations should be identified to ensure any limited scope project could easily integrate with larger enterprise architecture.

6.2.3   Vertical Scope

Vertical scope speaks to the level of detail appropriate to architecture effort. Time and resources may limit the amount of detail that a project should can handle; and the amount of detail appropriate will make demands on the time and resources required to complete the project.

Typically, the best approach to designing an enterprise is to document all models found within the enterprise to whatever level of detail is affordable. Future iterations of the architecture development cycle provide opportunities to add more detail to any particular model.

6.2.4   Time Period

Typically, the Architecture Development Method is described as a single cycle of Architecture Vision and a set of Target Architectures.

When the scope of the enterprise architecture is large or complex, a need exists to split the work to reach a Target Architecture into two or more discrete stages, specifically:

- Developing Target Architecture Descriptions for the overall system and demonstrating responses to stakeholder objectives and concerns over an extended timeframe.
- Developing one or more descriptions as increments and encompassing the overall Target Architecture description that presents the specific details of the increment concerned.

By definition, Target Architectures evolve and require periodic review and updates to incorporate any evolving business requirements and technology developments.

6.3 Preliminary Phase

The Preliminary phase of the Architecture Development Method is to prepare and initiate the activities required to meet a business directive within the enterprise architecture.

6.3.1 Preliminary Phase Objectives

The objectives of the Preliminary phase include:

- Reviewing the context of the organization fro conducting enterprise architecture development.
- Identifying the sponsor stakeholders and other major stakeholders who will be impacted by the business directive to create enterprise architecture and determine their requirements and concerns.
- Ensuring the commitment to the successful approach of the architecture process.
- Enabling the architecture sponsor to create requirements that effectively benefit all affected business areas.
- Identifying and scoping the elements of the enterprise and define the appropriate constraints and assumptions.
- Defining the people responsible for performing architecture work, where they are located and their responsibilities.
- Defining the framework and detailed methodologies to be

26

used in developing the enterprise architecture.
- Confirming a governance and support framework for providing business processes and resources.
- Selecting and implementing support tools for architecture activity.
- Defining the architecture principles that provide intended constraints on the architecture work.

6.3.2 Preliminary Phase Approach

The Preliminary Phase defines many of the general aspects of the architecture by defining
- The enterprise
- The key drivers and elements of the organization
- The requirements for architecture work
- The architecture principles
- The framework to be used
- The relationships between management frameworks
- The enterprise architecture maturity

6.3.3 Organizational Context

At first, architecture work revolves around identify general conditions for meeting strategic, tactical and interim objectives and expectations of the architecture. Scope becomes an immediate and highly important topic for defining the architecture work to be completed within the rest of the ADM cycle. A developed architecture is specific to a particular organization. The context derived by the organization is important to make effective and informed decisions about the framework. The areas of consideration in building the context include:

- Any commercial models for the architecture
- Budgetary plans for architecture activity
- The stakeholders and their key issues and concerns
- The intentions and culture of the organization
- Current projects supporting the execution of change and the operation of IT

- The Baseline Architecture landscape
- The skills and capabilities of the enterprise and encompassing organizations.

6.3.4   Requirements for Architecture Work

Business imperatives for the enterprise architecture are the primary drivers for any requirements to initiate work on the architecture. They are used to scope the work sufficiently. Requirements have a broad range, including:
- Business requirements
- Cultural aspirations
- Organizational intents
- Strategic intent
- Forecast financial requirements

6.3.5   Architecture Principles

Constraints are partially constructed by the business and architecture principles defined within the enterprise. Though business principles are normally formed outside the scope of the enterprise architecture work, they can be the basis for developing architecture principles.

Architecture governance has an important role in approving and enforcing architecture principles that have been adopted.

6.3.6   Management Frameworks

TOGAF is designed to work with other management frameworks that may be present in the current environment and even enhance their capabilities. Some other frameworks, which are recommended for use with TOGAF, include:
- Business Capability Management – determines the capabilities required to deliver business value
- Portfolio/Project Management Methods – determines the management of change initiatives

28

- Operations Management Methods - determines the activities of day-to-day operations
- Solution Development Methods – formalizes the process from which business systems are delivered.

6.3.7 Capability Maturity Model

Capability Maturity Models (CMMs) are used to assess specific factors within the environment with the intent of understanding how to develop and implement the architecture. They provide a level of maturity for the environment, which represents the organization/s ability to change and provides ways to improve that ability.

A broad range of enterprise characteristics are covered by an enterprise architecture maturity model. One such model, the NASCIO Enterprise Architecture Maturity Model, uses the following criteria:
- Administration – roles and responsibilities for governance
- Planning – program mashup and implementation plan
- Framework – processes and templates
- Blueprint – actual standards and specifications
- Communication – education and distribution of detail
- Compliance – adherence to standards, processes, and architecture elements
- Integration - management process interaction
- Involvement – support for the enterprise architecture program

6.3.8 Preliminary Phase Process

Inputs to the Preliminary phase come from external and internal sources to the enterprise and consist of architectural and non-architecture products. The expected inputs include:
- TOGAF and other architecture framework(s)
- Strategies and business plans
- Business principles, goals, and drivers
- Major frameworks currently implemented in the business
- Governance and legal frameworks
- Project budget for scoping

- Partnership and contract agreements
- IT strategy
- Pre-existing Architecture Framework, Organizational Model, and Architecture Repository

The steps of the Preliminary phase include:

1. Scoping the organizations impacted - identifying the enterprise units and communities directly affected (core), benefited (soft), and affected (extended) by the change as well as the governance involved.
2. Confirming the governance and support framework – the framework needs to exist and be adequate to establish the organizational change require to adopt a new enterprise architecture. This step ensures that framework is in place and the architecture touch-points and impact is understood and agreed upon by stakeholders.
3. Defining and establishing enterprise architecture team and organization -included determining the existing enterprise and business capability and maturity and defining the changes required to existing business programs and projects. The work required to perform this work and to resolve any gaps involved will determine the resources required for future work.
4. Identifying and establishing architecture principles – performed after establishing the organizational context.
5. Selecting and tailoring architecture framework – tailoring the framework focuses on the making appropriate adjustments to terminology, processes, and architectural content.
6. Implementing architecture tools – dependent on the scale, sophistication, and culture of the architecture function.

The outputs of the Preliminary phase are:

- Organizational Model for Enterprise Architecture
- Tailored Architecture Framework
- Initial Architecture Repository
- Restatement of business principles, goals, and drivers
- Request(s) for Architecture Work
- Governance Framework

The scope and goals of the Request for Architecture Work will define the level of detail to address in the phase. The steps involved in creating an Architecture Vision include:

1. Establishing the architecture project – the project may be part of a larger effort within the enterprise or be standalone.
2. Identifying stakeholders, concern, and business requirements – the purpose of engaging stakeholders is to identify stakeholder vision components and requirements, scope boundaries, concerns, issues, and cultural factors that may affect the effort.
3. Confirming business goals, drivers, and constraints
4. Evaluation business capabilities – using a business capability assessment, this step is used to understanding the realities of the organization to deliver on the target architecture and what is required to build up the organization's capabilities.
5. Assessing the business transformation readiness – In addition to the capabilities, the organization's ability to undergo a change in its architecture must be evaluated. The results of a readiness assessment can be used to scope the architecture project.
6. Defining scope – Specifically focusing on the breadth of coverage, level of detail, partitioning characteristics, covered architecture domains, extent of the time, and the leveraged architecture assets.
7. Confirming architecture and business principles
8. Developing the Architecture Vision – The Architecture Vision is developed as well as business scenarios for articulating that vision.
9. Defining the value propositions and KPIs of the Target Architecture – Develops the business case for the architecture, value propositions for each stakeholder grouping, assessing and defining the procurement requirements, defining the required performance metrics and measures, and assessing the business risk to the proposed Target Architecture.
10. Identifying the risk of business transformation and any mitigation activities – Identifying and classifying the initial and residual level of risk before and after mitigation.
11. Developing the Statement of Architecture Work – Ensures the proposed work products match the business performance requirements. Remaining activities seeks acceptance of the

Statement of Architecture Work by the sponsors and stakeholders.

The results of the Architecture Vision phase are:
- An approved Statement of Architecture Work
- Refined statements of business principles, goals, and strategic drivers
- Architecture principles
- Capability Assessment
- Tailored Architecture Framework
- Architecture Vision
- Communication Plan

6.5   Phase B: Business Architecture

The Business Architecture phase fo0cuses on the development of a business architecture that suitably supports the Architecture Vision that was agreed upon in the previous phase.

6.5.1   Business Architecture Phase Objectives

The objectives of the Business Architecture phase are to describe the Baseline Business Architecture and develop a Target business Architecture. Gaps between the baseline and target architectures are analyzed and the appropriate architecture viewpoints are selected and developed. The viewpoints assist in describing how the Business architecture addresses the relevant stakeholder concerns. The last objective of the phase is to identify the tools and techniques that will appropriately support the selected viewpoints.

6.5.2 Business Architecture Phase Approach

The business architecture is a prerequisite for work in any other architecture domain and it the first set of activities to be complete in developing the overall enterprise architecture. Business value and return on investment in architecture activity can be demonstrated to stakeholders because the business architecture is defined appropriately from the very start.

The scope of the Phase B work is dependent on the level of detail already available within the enterprise environment. In some cases, the activity is simply to confirm and update the existing business strategies and plans to bridge between those strategies, goals, and strategic drivers to the specific business requirements related to the architecture development effort. In other cases, the architecture team will have to perform extensive research, verification, and consensus building over key business objectives and processes, which the architecture is intended to support. The key objective of the Business Architecture phase is to re-use as much existing material as possible.

Architecture descriptions are used to develop the Baseline Description of the enterprise architecture. The development of the Baseline Description involves a bottom-up analysis of the current state of the environment. During the analysis, the intrinsic values of architecture components are determine. However, some of these components may not be used in developing the Baseline Description, knowledge and understanding of these components is necessary especially in determining the any residual value that may exist in including or not including them.

6.5.3   Architecture Modeling

Business scenarios may be created to demonstrate the value of the architecture to the business. A logical extension of these scenarios is the business model, which maps the high-level business requirements to low-level requirements. Several forms of modeling tools and techniques may be utilized to perform this mapping, including:

- Business Process (or Activity) Models – describes the functions related to business activities, data, and communication between activities.
- Use-Case Models – describes processes or functions as they apply to specific scenarios in order to describe the relationships between business processes and organizational participants.
- Class Models – describes static information and their relations and behaviors.

These model types are typically represented in the Unified Modeling Language (UML). Some industry sectors have specific modeling techniques used in their sector, such as:

- Node Connectivity Diagram – describes the business location (nodes), the conceptual, logical, and physical connections and the characteristics in exchanged information.
- Information Exchange Matrix – documents the information exchange requirements for enterprise architecture, specifically activities, business nodes, and information flow. Information exchange characteristics such as performance and security are the some of the focus areas of the matrix.

6.5.4   Architecture Repository

The Architecture Repository provides storage for relevant resources useful in developing architecture for any of the four domains. For the business architecture, the relevant resources include generic business models within the organization's industry, or "industry architectures," or models related to common high-level business domains such as e-commerce or supply change management. Enterprise-specific building blocks and applicable standard can also be found within the Architecture Repository.

6.5.5   Business Architecture Phase Process

The expected inputs to the Business Architecture Phase include:
- Architecture reference materials from external sources
- Request for Architecture Work
- Business principles, goals and strategic drivers
- Capability Assessment
- Communications Plan
- Organizational Model for Enterprise Architecture
- Tailored Architecture Frameworks
- Approved Statement of Architecture Work
- Architecture and business principles
- Enterprise Continuum
- Architecture Repository
- Architecture Vision

One of the focuses of the Business Architecture phase is adequately defining business processes in the detail required to support the architecture. This is especially true for new business processes that are introduced. The general steps of the phase include:
1. Selecting reference models, viewpoints, and tools – Provides the basis for developing, demonstrating, and communicating the business architecture and includes identifying the overall modeling process, the requirement service granularity, boundaries, and contracts, and the catalogs of relevant business building blocks, matrices, and diagrams. The types of requirements to be collected are also determined.

2. Developing the Baseline Business Architecture Description – Provides a current outlook on the existing business environment. Using the information discovered in the previous step can aid in developing the description.
3. Developing the Target Business Architecture Description - provides a future representation of the business architecture suitable to meet the new architecture requirements.
4. Performing gap analysis – Identifies the gaps between the baseline and target architecture. In the process, will resolve conflicts using trade-off analysis, validate that models support the principles, objectives, and constraints, and test for completeness in the architecture models.
5. Defining roadmap components – Aids in prioritizing activities in subsequent phases.
6. Resolving impact – Aids in determining the impact of implementing the target business architecture in the current environment and the ongoing activities of enterprise operations.
7. Conducting formal reviews – Ensures that target business architecture meets the requirements of the stakeholders.
8. Finalizing the Business Architecture – Selects the building blocks and the appropriate standards for those building blocks, as well as any supporting work products.
9. Creating the Architecture Definition Document – used to document the rationale for building block decisions and providing a description of several components of the business architecture, including:
   - A business footprint
   - A management footprint
   - Business functions and information needs
   - Any relevant standards, rules and guidelines
   - A skills matrix and associated job descriptions

The outputs of the Business Architecture Phase include:
   - Refinement of Architecture Vision phase deliverables
   - Draft version of the Architecture Definition Document including the baseline and target business architecture
   - Draft Architecture Requirements Specification
   - Business Architecture components

6.6 Phase C: Information Systems Architectures

The Information Systems Architectures include the development of Data and Application Architectures.

6.6.1 Information Systems Architectures Objectives

The primary objective of the Information Systems Architectures phase is to develop the Target Architectures for either or both the data and application systems domains. This includes identifying and defining the data and application considerations for supporting the business architecture that was developed in the previous phase.

6.6.2 Data and Application Architecture Objectives

The objectives related to data architectures refer to defining the major types and sources of data to support the business such that the data is understandable by stakeholders, complete and consistent, and stable. Database design is not a concern of designing data architectures, but rather to define the data entities relevant to the enterprise.

The objectives related to application architectures refer to defining the major kinds of application systems required to process the data and support the business. Application systems design is not a concern of designing the application architectures, just the types of application systems relevant to the enterprise and the requirements placed on those systems to manage and present information. In this sense, applications are logical groups of capabilities managing data objects, not computer systems.

6.6.3 Information Systems Architectures Approach

The approach used to develop information systems architectures utilizes tools and techniques for developing data and application architectures, including Enterprise Architecture Planning (ERP), Enterprise Resource Planning (ERP), and Customer Relationship

Management (CRM). The focus of the architecture effort is on the implementation and integration of core applications for mission-critical business processes.

Implementation of architecture is commonly approached by designing top-down and performing a bottoms-up implementation, though the steps for implementing can follow any order. Another approach is data driven; where applications systems that create data are first implemented, then applications, which process data, and then application that archive data.

6.6.4 Data and Application Architectures Approach

Designing the Data Architecture considers the following aspects:
- Data Management – addressing any guidelines, concerns, and solutions that lead to a structured and comprehensive approach to data management.
- Data Migration – identifying the requirements for migrating when existing applications are replaced.
- Data Governance – ensuring the enterprise capabilities enable transformation through the structure, management systems and personnel required to manage data.

The Architecture Repository may provide relevant resources to develop the target architecture, particularly in the form of generic business, data, and application models.

6.6.5 Information Systems Architectures Process

The general inputs to the Information Systems Architecture include:
- Request for Architecture Work
- Capability Assessment
- Communications Plan
- Organization Model for Enterprise Architecture
- Tailored Architecture Framework
- Application principles
- Data principles
- Statement of Architecture Work

40

- Architecture Vision
- Architecture Repository
- Draft Architecture Definition Document
- Baseline and Target Architectures for Business, Data, and Application
- Draft Architecture Requirements Specification
- Architecture Roadmap, specifically related to the business architecture

Specific steps are associated with both data and application architecture domains. In either case, the level of detail required is dependent on the scope and goals of the overall effort. Building blocks, whether new or existing, must be defined within this phase.

The specific steps related to developing the data architecture are:
1. Selecting reference models, viewpoints, and tools – Provides the basis for developing, demonstrating, and communicating the data architecture and includes reviewing and validating data principles, selecting relevant resources and viewpoints, and tools and techniques for data capture, modeling and analysis. Identifying the overall modeling process for each viewpoint, and the catalogs of relevant data building blocks, matrices, and diagrams are important steps at the very start, particularly:
   - Data Entity/Data Component catalog
   - Data Entity/Business Function matrix
   - Business Service/Information matrix
   - System/Data matrix
   - Class diagram
   - Data Dissemination diagram
   - Data Lifecycle diagram
   - Data Security diagram
   - Data Migration diagram
   - Class Hierarchy diagram
2. Developing the Baseline Data Architecture Description – Provides a current outlook on the existing business environment. Using the information discovered in the Architecture Vision phase can aid in developing the description.

3. Developing the Target Data Architecture Description - provides a future representation of the data architecture suitable to meet the new architecture requirements.
4. Performing gap analysis – Identifies the gaps between the baseline and target architecture. In the process, will resolve conflicts using trade-off analysis, validate that models support the principles, objectives, and constraints, and test for completeness in the architecture models.
5. Defining roadmap components – Aids in prioritizing activities in subsequent phases.
6. Resolving impact – Aids in determining the impact of implementing the target data architecture in the current environment and the ongoing activities of enterprise operations.
7. Conducting formal reviews – Ensures that target data architecture meets the requirements of the stakeholders.
8. Finalizing the Data Architecture – Selects the building blocks and the appropriate standards for those building blocks, as well as any supporting work products.
9. Creating the Architecture Definition Document – used to document the rationale for building block decisions and providing a description of several components of the data architecture, including:
   • Business data model
   • Logical data model
   • Data management process model
   • Data Entity/Business Function matrix
   • Data Interoperability requirements

The specific steps related to developing the application architecture are:
1. Selecting reference models, viewpoints, and tools – Provides the basis for developing, demonstrating, and communicating the application architecture and includes reviewing and validating application principles, selecting relevant resources and viewpoints, and tools and techniques for data capture, modeling and analysis. The types of requirements to be collected are determined. Identifying the overall modeling process for each viewpoint, and the catalogs of relevant data building blocks, matrices, and diagrams are important steps at the very start, particularly:

42

- Application Portfolio catalog
- Interface catalogs
- System/Organization matrix
- Role/System matrix
- Application Interaction matrix
- System/Function matrix
- Application Communication diagram
- Application and User Location diagram
- Enterprise Manageability diagram
- Process/System Realization diagram
- Application Migration diagram
- Software Distribution diagram
- Software Engineering diagram

2. Developing the Baseline Application Architecture Description – Provides a current outlook on the existing business environment. Using the information discovered in the Architecture Vision phase can aid in developing the description.

3. Developing the Target Application Architecture Description - provides a future representation of the data architecture suitable to meet the new architecture requirements.

4. Performing gap analysis – Identifies the gaps between the baseline and target architecture. In the process, will resolve conflicts using trade-off analysis, validate that models support the principles, objectives, and constraints, and test for completeness in the architecture models.

5. Defining roadmap components – Aids in prioritizing activities in subsequent phases.

6. Resolving impact – Aids in determining the impact of implementing the target application architecture in the current environment and the ongoing activities of enterprise operations.

7. Conducting formal reviews – Ensures that target application architecture meets the requirements of the stakeholders.

8. Finalizing the Application Architecture – Selects the building blocks and the appropriate standards for those building blocks, as well as any supporting work products.

9. Creating the Architecture Definition Document – used to document the rationale for building block decisions and providing a description of several components of the application architecture.

43

The primary outputs of the Information Systems Architecture are:
- Refining the Architecture Vision
- Drafting the Architecture Definition Document for Data and Application Architectures
- Drafting the Data and Application sections of the Architecture Requirements Specification
- Identifying the information system components of an Architecture Roadmap

6.7 Phase D: Technology Architecture

The Technology Architecture phase of the Architecture Development Method focuses on the technical aspects of the enterprise architecture

6.7.1 Technology Architecture Objectives

In more specific terms, the Technology Architecture phase provides an opportunity to map application components into a set of hardware and software components configured into a technology platform. Because the phase defines the physical realization of the overall architecture, the phase has strong connections to implementation and migration planning. The baseline and target views of the technology portfolio are defined to determine the Target Architecture.

6.7.2 Technology Architecture Approach

As with the previous phases, the Architecture Repository provides an excellent source for obtaining relevant Technology Architecture components that already exist, specifically:
- Existing IT services
- TOGAF Technical Reference Model (TRM)
- Generic technology models
- Technology models relevant to Common Systems Architectures

The decisions made in previous phases of the Architecture Development Method may have implications on the technology components and platform, particularly those decisions around service granularity and service boundaries. The areas of impact within the Technology Architecture include:

- Performance – platform service requirements can contain services with several functionality units that with varying non-functional requirements and more services than required by the requesting system
- Maintainability – If service granularity is to general, the introduction of change to the system may be too difficult and costly.
- Location and Latency – Inter-service communication may be impacted by the inappropriate setting of service boundaries and granularity
- Availability – When defining service composition and service granularity, high availability concerns may be a key determiner.

Product selection is important in offsetting the impact in these areas and builds technology architecture suitable to support the enterprise.

6.7.3   Technology Architecture Process

The expected inputs to the Technology Architecture Phase include:

- Architecture reference materials from external sources
- Product information
- Request for Architecture Work
- Capability Assessment
- Communications Plan
- Organizational Model for Enterprise Architecture
- Tailored Architecture Frameworks
- Approved Statement of Architecture Work
- Technology principles
- Architecture Repository
- Draft Architecture Definition Document
- Draft Architecture Requirements Specifications
- Business, Data, and Application Architecture components of the Architecture Roadmap.

One of the focuses of the Technology Architecture phase is adequately defining technology building blocks, existing and new, in the detail required to support the architecture. The general steps of the phase include:

1. Selecting reference models, viewpoints, and tools – Provides the basis for developing, demonstrating, and communicating the technology architecture and identifying the overall modeling process, service portfolios, boundaries, and contracts, and the catalogs of relevant business building blocks, matrices, and diagrams, particularly:
   - Technology standards catalog
   - Technology portfolio catalog
   - System/Technology matrix
   - Environments and Locations diagram
   - Platform Decomposition diagram
   - Processing diagram
   - Networked Computing/Hardware diagram
   - Communications Engineering diagram
2. Developing the Baseline Technology Architecture Description – Provides a current outlook on the existing technical environment. Using the information discovered in the previous step can aid in developing the description.
3. Developing the Target Technology Architecture Description - provides a future representation of the technology architecture suitable to meet the new architecture requirements.
4. Performing gap analysis – Identifies the gaps between the baseline and target architecture. In the process, will resolve conflicts using trade-off analysis, validate that models support the principles, objectives, and constraints, and test for completeness in the architecture models.
5. Defining roadmap components – Aids in prioritizing activities in subsequent phases.
6. Resolving impact – Aids in determining the impact of implementing the target technology architecture in the current environment and the ongoing activities of enterprise operations.
7. Conducting formal reviews – Ensures that target technology architecture meets the requirements of the stakeholders.
8. Finalizing the Technology Architecture – Selects the building blocks and the appropriate standards for those building

46

blocks, as well as any supporting work products.

9. Creating the Architecture Definition Document – used to document the rationale for building block decisions and providing a description of several components of the technology architecture, including:
   - Functionality and attributes
   - Dependent building blocks
   - Interfaces
   - Mapping to business and organizational entities and policies

The outputs of the Business Architecture Phase include:
- Refinement of Architecture Vision phase deliverables
- Draft version of the Architecture Definition Document including the baseline and target technology architecture
- Draft Architecture Requirements Specification
- Technology Architecture components

6.8 Phase E: Opportunities and Solutions

The Opportunities and Solutions phase describes the process for identifying projects, programs, and portfolios that effectively deliver the Target Architectures developed in the previous phases of the ADM.

6.8.1 Opportunities and Solutions Objectives

The objectives of the Opportunities and Solutions are:
- Review the target business objectives and capabilities, consolidate the gaps from the previous phases and organize into groups to address the capabilities.
- Review and confirm the current parameters of the enterprise to absorb change.
- Create a series of incremental Transition Architectures to deliver business value while exploiting opportunities.
- Generate and gain consensus on the Implementation and Migration Strategy.

47

6.8.2 Opportunities and Solutions Approach

The Opportunities and Solutions phase is where the architecture team starts to be concerned with the actual implementation of the Target Architecture, looking into best path for implementing the architecture, bot h from the corporate business and technical perspective. IT activities are logically grouped into project work packages.

From an enterprise strategic change perspective, opportunities and solutions are identifying from top-down based on the architecture work already performed. Because identify existing opportunities and solutions is a key function of this phase, the list of inputs is extensive and the information provide often has to e consolidated, integrated, and analyzed sufficiently to identify the best way to proceed.

Key to implementation, the issues related to co-existence and interoperability are examined and clarified. Within this perspective, the risks to implementation are identified, consolidated, and accepted pragmatically, transferred, or mitigated.

6.8.3 Implementation and Migration Strategy

At this point, an implementation and migration strategy is created to outline the critical path of the overall implementation approach. This strategy is supported by the results of dependency analysis where the requirements of specific work packages are identified and related to other work packages to isolate the critical path. These work packages are then organized into portfolios, projects, and initiatives by the architecture.

The architectures for previous phases are used to develop a series of Transition Architecture to obtain an incremental progress to the Target Architecture.

6.8.4 Transition Architecture

The size and complexity of the gap between the baseline and target
architectures will decide the number of increments realistically
possible to move the architecture from the baseline to the target.
Each of these increments is considered a Transition Architecture and
consists of sets of co-ordinated and defined building blocks grouped
into work packages. Transition Architectures allow changes to
architecture without too extensive of impact on the organization in any
single increment. It also allows simultaneous work on several
architectures to be conducted on different levels of detail.

6.8.5 Opportunities and Solutions Process

The inputs of the Opportunities and Solutions phase include:
- Architecture reference materials
- Product information
- Request for Architecture Work
- Capability Assessment
- Communications Plan
- Planning methodologies
- Organizational Model for Enterprise Architecture
- Governance models and frameworks
- Tailored Architecture Framework
- Statement of Architecture Work
- Architecture Vision
- Architecture Repository
- Draft Architecture Definition Document
- Draft Architecture Requirements Specification
- Change Requests

The steps of the Opportunities and Solutions phase are:
1. Determining key corporate change attributes – ties in the
   organization's business culture to the best implementation
   approach for the enterprise architecture and includes the
   creation of an Implementation Factor Assessment and
   Deduction Matrix to store all architecture implementation and
   migration decisions.

49

2. Determining business constraints – identifies the business drivers that may constrain the sequence of implementation activities and includes a review of the corporate and corporate live-of-business strategic plans and the Enterprise Architecture Maturity Assessment.
3. Consolidating gap analysis results – consolidates and integrates the gap analysis results from the Business, Information Systems, and Technology Architectures and creates the Consolidated Gaps, Solutions, and Dependencies Matrix to easily find SBBs to address one or more gaps
4. Reviewing IT requirements – assessing the IT requirements, gaps, solutions, and factors with the intent to find the minimum set of functional requirements to implement the Target Architecture more effectively and efficiently.
5. Consolidating interoperability requirements – Uses the requirements found int eh previous phases to consolidate and reconcile the interoperability requirements.
6. Validating dependencies – identifies the business, information, workflow, IT, and Foundation dependencies as they relate to constraints on the Implementation and Migration Plans.
7. Confirming readiness and risk for business transformation – assess the organization's readiness to handle the business transformation changes and adapt to the associated risks.
8. Formulating Implementation and Migration Strategy – identifies the strategic approach to introduce the new architecture into the existing environment. Generally, there are three basic approaches:
   - Greenfield – starting from the beginning
   - Revolutionary – radical change to the environment
   - Evolutionary – phased approach to introduce capabilities
   Implementation planning attempt to identify quick wins, achievable targets, and value chain methods.
9. Grouping major work packages – major work packages are identified, analyzed, and classified as mainstream, contain, and replace systems.
10. Identifying Transition Architectures – When an incremental approach is required to realize the Target Architecture, Transition Architectures and Capabilities are identified

11. Creating portfolio and project charters – Each incremental work effort must have appropriate project documentation in place to move forward to realize the Transition and Target Architectures

The expected outputs of the Opportunities and Solutions phase include:

- Refined versions of the Architecture Vision, Business, Information Systems, and Technology Architecture deliverables
- Consolidated Architecture Roadmap
- Capability Assessment
- Transition Architecture(s)
- Implementation and Migration Plan

6.9   Phase F: Migration Planning

The Migration Planning phase focuses on the development of an Implementation and Migration Plan, which realizes the Transition Architectures from the previous phase in part, or in whole.

6.9.1   Migration Planning Objectives

The objectives of Migration Planning concentrate on finalizing the Implementation and Migration Plan, particularly:

- Ensuring the Implementation and Migration Plan co-ordinates with other management frameworks in use within the enterprise.
- Prioritizing work packages, projects, and building blocks through assigned business value and cost/benefit analysis.
- Finalizing the Architecture Vision and Architecture Definition Documents to align with the implementation approach.
- Confirming the Transition Architectures with stakeholders

- Creating, evolving, and monitoring the detailed Implementation and Migration Plan

6.9.2 Migration Planning Approach

The primary focus of the Migration Planning approach is to create a viable Implementation and Migration Plan with the assigned portfolio and project managers. This includes assessing the dependencies, costs and benefits of the transition architecture and migration projects.

The Implementation and Migration Plan is just one part of a series of plans issued by the enterprise management frameworks that must be co-ordinated with deliver business value and ensure resources are available when required. The Migration Planning phase ensures that all concerned organizational agencies are fully aware of the scope and adopt the Implementation and Migration Plan appropriately with their current activities. Additionally. the architecture evolution cycle is established to ensure relevancy of the architecture in the midst of business and technological advancement.

6.9.3 Migration Planning Process

The inputs to the Migration Planning phase include:
- Architecture reference materials
- Requests for Architecture Work
- Capability Assessment
- Communications Plan
- Organizational Model for Enterprise Architecture
- Governance models and frameworks
- Tailored Architecture Framework
- Statement of Architecture Work
- Architecture Vision
- Architecture Repository
- Draft Architecture Definition Document
- Draft Architecture Requirements Specification
- Change Requests
- Consolidated Architecture Roadmap

- Transition Architectures
- Implementation and Migration Plan

The steps of the phase are:
1. Confirming management framework interactions – Working through the Implementation and Migration Plan to co-ordinate and align activities with other frameworks, particularly Business Planning, Enterprise Architecture, Portfolio/Project Management, and Operations Management.
2. Assigning business value to each project – addresses various issues to ensure business value parameters are understood and utilized, including:
   - Performance Evaluation Criteria
   - Return on Investment Criteria
   - Business Value
   - Critical Success Factors
   - Measures of Effectiveness
   - Strategic Fit
3. Estimating requirements, timings, and vehicles – Determine the resource requirements, times for executing each project or project increment and provide initial cost estimates for each project. This includes the availability and delivery of the resources for each project.
4. Prioritizing migration projects – Using cost/benefit analysis and risk validation to identify the benefits and each project and determine the appropriate priority.
5. Confirming Transition Architecture Increments – Updates the Architecture Definition Document with updated information about the transition architecture(s).
6. Generating the Architecture Implementation Roadmap – Establishes the sequencing of the Implementation and Migration Plan to ensure consistent adding of business value through the transition architecture projects being executed in a timely and effective basis.
7. Establishing the architecture evolution cycle – Manages the Enterprise Architectures and Transition Architecture as configuration items that are maintained and evolved throughout the lifecycle of the varied solutions.

The expected outputs of the Migration Planning phase consist of:
- Implementation and Migration Plan
- Finalized Architecture Definition Document
- Finalized Architecture Requirements Specification m
- Finalized Architecture Roadmap
- Finalized Transition Architecture
- Re-usavble Architecture Building Blocks
- Requests for Architecture Work
- Architecture Contracts
- Implementation Governance Model
- Change Requests

6.10 Phase G: Implementation Governance

The Implementation Governance phase provides architectural oversight of the implementation.

6.10.1 Implementation Governance Objectives

The objectives of the Implementation Governance phase are:
- To formulate recommendations for each implementation project.
- To govern and manage Architecture Contract(s) covering the implementation and deployment process.
- To perform any required governance functions during implementation or deployment.
- To ensure conformance to the defined architectures.
- To ensure conformance of the deployed solutions to the Target Architecture.
- To ensure the solutions are deployed successfully.
- To mobilize operations to support lifecycle success of the deployed solutions.

6.10.2 Implementation Governance Approach

The approach used by the Implementation Governance phase is to establish an implementation program to enable the delivery of transition architectures agreed upon in the Migration Planning phase and a phased deployment schedule based on business priorities and guided by the Architecture Roadmap.

The corporate, IT, and architecture governance standards adopted by the organization should be followed at all times, as well as any established portfolio, program management approach that may exist. The operations framework required to ensure an effective life of the deployed solution is also defined.

Using the Architecture Contract, the implementation and architecture organizations are connected.

6.10.3 Implementation Governance Process

The inputs to the Implementation Governance phase include:
- Architecture reference materials
- Request for Architecture Work
- Capacity Assessment
- Organizational Model for Enterprise Architecture
- Tailored Architecture Framework
- Statement of Architecture Work
- Architecture Vision
- Architectures Repository
- Architecture Definition Document
- Architecture Requirements Specification
- Architecture Roadmap
- Transition Architectures
- Implementation Governance Model
- Architecture Contract
- Implementation and Migration Plan

The steps of the Implementation Governance phase consist of:

1. Confirming scope and priorities for deployment – review the outputs of migration planning and produce recommendation. Identify priorities, issues, and building blocks and perform gap analysis related to Solution Building Blocks.
2. Identifying deployment resources and skills – identify the system development methods required to develop solution and ensure the method allows feedback to be given to the architecture team on designs.
3. Guiding development of solutions deployment – formulates recommendations on the project, document the Architecture Contract and update any documentation or repositories.
4. Performing compliance reviews – Review the current governance and compliance for each building block and conduct post-development reviews with the intention of closing the development portion of the deployment projects.
5. Implementing business and IT operations - carry out each deployment project, ensuring that all new Baseline Architectures are published to the Architecture Repository and other repositories impacted are updated.
6. Performing post implementation review – conduct all reviews after implementation, publishing those reviews and closing out projects as they complete.

The expected outputs of the Implementation Governance phase include:

- Architecture Contract
- Compliance Assessments
- Change Requests
- Architecture-compliant solutions

6.11 Phase H: Architecture Change Management

The Architecture Change Management phase concentrates on the managing the changes specific to the architectures created in Phases A through D.

6.11.1 Architecture Change Management Objectives

The objectives of the Architecture Change Management phase are:
- Ensure that baseline architectures maintain fit-for-purpose characteristics.
- Assess the performance of the architecture and make recommendations for change
- Assess changes to the framework and principles
- Establish a process for architecture change management for the new enterprise architecture baseline
- Maximize the business value from the architecture and operations
- Operate the Governance Framework

6.11.2 Architecture Change Management Approach

An Architecture Change Management process can ensure the business value expected from architecture is maintained. The process does this by managing changes to the architecture and monitoring governance requests, new development in technology, and changes in the business environment. When changes are identified, the process will determine whether to initiate a formal request within the architecture evolution cycle.

Several aspects of the architecture can influence change, such as continual use of the architecture, capacity measurements and performance management. Change management provides guidance on the situations where changes to the enterprise architecture will be allowed after deployment and the situations where a new architecture development cycle will be initiated. When change is required in the architecture, the process ensures the work products of the change comply with the established enterprise architecture.

6.11.3 Drivers for Change

Changes to the existing infrastructure can be integrated with the enterprise architecture in the following ways:
- Strategically form a top down approach with directed changes to enhance or create new capabilities
- Bottom up changes to correct or enhance capability from operations management
- From experiences with previously delivered project that are in the care of operations management and delivered outside this function

An Architecture Board will typically assess and approve all Requests for Change (RFC) to the architecture. The reasons for changes requests generally come from technology or business reasons. Business reasons for change are a result of:
- Business-as-usual developments
- Business exceptions
- Business innovations
- Business technology innovations
- Strategic changes

The technological reasons include:
- New technology reports
- Asset management cost reductions
- Technology withdrawal
- Initiatives related to standards

6.11.4 Architecture Change Management Process

The Change Management process determines how changes are managed and the techniques and methodologies used. Changes range for maintenance activities to architecture re-design. Architectural changes are classified into three categories:

- Simplification change
- Incremental change
- Re-architecting change

Determining the category of a change requires that:

- All events impacting the architecture are registered
- Architecture tasks are properly resources and managed
- Assessment of activity by responsible party managing resources
- Evaluation of impact to the architecture

The inputs to the Architecture Change Management phase include:

- Architecture reference materials
- Requests for Architecture Work
- Organizational Model for Enterprise Architecture
- Tailored Architecture Framework
- Statement of Architecture Work
- Architecture Vision
- Architecture Repository
- Architecture Definition Document
- Architecture Requirements Specification
- Architecture Roadmap
- Change Request for technology or business change
- Transition Architecture
- Implementation Governance Model
- Architecture Contract
- Compliance Assessments
- Implementation and Migration Plan

The steps related to the Architecture Change Management phase are:

1. Establishing value realization process – Exploits value realization within business projects.
2. Deploying monitoring tools – Used to track a variety of influencing aspects, such as:
   - Technology changes
   - Business changes
   - Enterprise architecture capability maturity
   - Asset management
   - QoS performances
   - business continuity requirements
3. Managing risk – Manages the architecture risks and provides recommendations for IT strategy.
4. Providing analysis – Analyses performance, conducts performance reviews, assesses change requests, and performs gap analysis to ensure that changes conform to the enterprise architecture governance and framework.
5. Developing change requirements - Making recommendation on change requirements.
6. Managing governance process – Manage Architecture Board meetings.
7. Activating the process to implement change – produces a new Request for Architecture Work and ensures work products of changes are captured int eh Architecture Repository

The output s of the Architecture Change Management phase is:
- Updates to the Architecture for maintenance reasons
- Changes to the architecture framework and principles
- New Request for Architecture Work
- Statement of Architecture Work
- Architecture Contract
- Compliance Assessments

Copyright The Art of Service | Brisbane, Australia | Email:service@theartofservice.com
Web: http://theartofservice.com | eLearning: http://theartofservice.org | Phone: +61 (0)7 3252 2055

6.12 Architecture Requirements Management

Architecture Requirements Management provides a process for managing architecture requirements throughout the Architecture Development Method.

6.12.1 Requirements Management Objectives

The objective of the Requirements Management phase is to define a process where requirements for the enterprise architecture can be identified, stored, and fed through the relevant ADM phases.

6.12.2 Requirements Management Approach

The requirements management phase continuously drives the ADM and represents a dynamic process for handling requirements through the ADM.

TOGAF does not recommend or endorse a particular requirements management tool, just what an effective requirements management process should be expected to achieve. Some common tools include:
- Business Scenarios
- Volere Requirements Specification Template
- Commercial Off-The-Shelf (COTS) tools

6.12.3 Requirements Management Process

The inputs to the Requirements Management phase are:
- Updated Architecture Repository
- Organizational Model for Enterprise Architecture
- Tailored Architecture Framework
- Statement of Architecture Work
- Architecture Vision
- Architecture requirements
- Requirements Impact Assessment

The steps of the Requirements Management phase are cooperation between requirement management and other ADM phases, and include:

1. Identify document requirements – From various ADM phases using business scenarios or analogous techniques.
2. Determining baseline requirements – Includes determining priorities, confirming stakeholders, and recording the requirements in the requirements repository.
3. Monitoring baseline requirements.
4. Identifying changed requirements – remove and add priorities and or requirements through ADM phases
5. Identifying changed requirements – specific steps through the requirements management process to identify change requirements and create new priorities. Identify any conflicts and generate Requirements Impact Statement.
6. Assess Impact on current and previous phases and create a Requirements Impact Statement.
7. Implement requirements
8. Document or update requirements repository.
9. Implement change in the current phase.
10. Assess and revise gap analysis for past phases.

The output of the requirements management process consists of:

- Requirements Impact Assessment
- Updated Architecture Requirements Specification
- Updated Requirements Repository

7   Adapting the Architecture Development Method

The Architecture Development Method can be used in variety scenarios that differ in process styles or architectures requirements.

7.1   Applying Iteration

The Architecture Development Method is a process that can be used with other development or project management methods or as a stand-alone process. To support this flexibility, the ADM can be used iteratively. The factors to influence to what extent the method is iterative are:
- Formality and nature of established process checkpoints
- Level of stakeholder information
- Number of teams involved
- Maturity of the deployed solutions
- Attitude to risk

Iteration is characterized within ADM as:
- Allowing project teams to cycle through the entire ADM because of Architecture Change Management.
- Allowing project teams to cycle between ADM phases in planned cycles covering multiple phases.
- Allowing project teams to operate ADM cycles concurrently with relationships between different teams.

7.1.1   Iteration Cycles

Iteration cycles span multiple phases of activity and allow formal review when each iteration cycle is complete. The suggested iteration cycles are:
- Architecture Context Iteration – initial architecture activity that establish approach, principles, scope, and vision.
- Architecture Definition Iteration – creates the architecture content through the Business, Information system, and Technology Architecture phases.
- Transition Planning Iteration – creates formal change roadmaps for the defined architectures.

63

Copyright The Art of Service | Brisbane, Australia | Email:service@theartofservice.com
Web: http://theartofservice.com | eLearning: http://theartofservice.org | Phone: +61 (0)7 3252 2055

- Architecture Governance Iterations – manages change activity while reaching for a defined Target Architecture.

An important first step is defining the architecture. Two process styles to do this exist:
- Baseline First – baseline assessments assist in identifying problem areas and improvement opportunities and useful when target solutions are not understood and agreed upon.
- Target First – the target solution is defined further and mapped back to the baseline description to identify the required change activity.

Combining the two concepts above, the activities found in each iteration generally follow as such:
- Architecture Context – encompasses the initial iteration to establish the approach, principles, scope, and vision for the engagement and utilizes the Preliminary and Architecture Vision phases.
- Architecture Definition for Baseline First styles – multiple iterations with the first iteration focusing on defining the Baseline Architecture and utilizes the Business, Information, and Technology Architecture phases.
  The second iteration defines the Target Architecture and gaps to the baseline and utilizes the Business, Information, and Technology Architecture phases.
  Any subsequent iteration will refine the baseline and target architectures and gaps between the two with the intent to achieve a beneficial, feasible, and viable outcome.
- Architecture Definition for Target First styles – multiple iterations with the first iteration focusing on defining the Target Architecture and utilizes the Business, Information, and Technology Architecture phases.
  The second iteration defines the Baseline Architecture and gaps to the baseline and utilizes the Business, Information, and Technology Architecture phases.
  Any subsequent iteration will refine the baseline and target architectures and gaps between the two with the intent to achieve a beneficial, feasible, and viable outcome.

Copyright The Art of Service | Brisbane, Australia | Email:service@theartofservice.com
Web: http://theartofservice.com | eLearning: http://theartofservice.org | Phone: +61 (0)7 3252 2055

- Transition Planning – in the first iteration will define and obtain agreement for a set of improvement opportunities aligns with a provisional Transition Architecture and utilizes the Opportunities, Solution phase, and Migration Planning phase to create a provisional plan. Subsequent iterations aim to agree to a Transition Architecture with refined improvement opportunities associated to it. Refinement of the migration plans and opportunities and solutions are expected.
- Architecture Governance – the first iteration focuses on the mobilization of the architecture governance and change management across the enterprise with subsequent iterations maintaining governance and change control.

7.1.2 Different Enterprise Levels

The TOGAF Architecture Development Method (ADM) can support the definition and implementation of architecture at different levels throughout the enterprise. To do this, the enterprise is partitioned based on subject matter, time, and level of detail.

From the different partitions, the architects may be engaged for a variety of reasons, the three most typically being:
- Identifying Required Changes – used to provide visibility of IT capabilities to support decision-making and alignment of execution.
- Defining Changes – after identify a need for change, architecture can be used to define the nature and extent of the change. A detailed Architecture Definition for change initiatives can be developed.
- Implementing Changes – Architects can provide governance to change initiations through big-picture visibility, supplying structural constraints, and defining criteria for evaluating decisions.

Different architectures can be address different stakeholder needs. Though they have a different focus from each other, none exists in isolation and sits within the governance hierarchy.

The strategies used to enable the ADM to support hierarchies of architectures consist of:

- Developing architectures through iterations within a single cycle of the ADM process.
- Developing architectures through a hierarchy of ADM processes, which are executed concurrently.

The single ADM cycle is typically used when a single architecture team is tasked with defining the multiple architectures. The Architecture Visions phase is used to provide a strategic view o the architecture, while the architecture development phases (B, C, and D) provide detail and formal views to the architecture for different segment or times.

The single cycle approach is lightweight, allows very close integration of architectures, and with work well when a single architecture team is responsible for development. Unfortunately, it is limited because governance and change management relationships between different architectures are not explicitly set, the architectures have to be completed in sequence and may even have to be released at the same time, and since similar architecture actives are repeated through the same phases, differences are often indistinguishable.

Large-scale architectures usually have multiple architecture teams involved and require a hierarchical application of the ADM. This approach is comprehensive and explicitly sets the governance relationships between the architectures, and allows for federated development of architectures. The limitations of the approach consist of a requirement for effective establishment of governance hierarchy and works well when multiple teams of architectures are utilized.

7.2 Security Architectures

Development of security architecture typically has a dual perception of remaining separate from the rest of the enterprise architecture development and needing to be integrated with that enterprise architecture. The security architect is tasked with the enforcement of security policies, including within the new developments of the enterprise architecture.

Security architectures have the following characteristics:

- They have their own methods.
- They have their own discrete views and viewpoints.
- They address non-normative flows.
- They introduce their own normative flows.
- They introduce unique, single purpose components
- They require a unique set of skill requirements in the IT architect

The concerns of the security architect include:
- Authentication
- Authorization
- Audit
- Assurance
- Availability
- Asset Protection
- Administration
- Risk Management

The enterprise requirements management process should include the security policy and standards. The security policy is an executive creation and is generally long-term entities in the enterprise. Standards, however, change more frequently and are often tied to specific technologies. New security requirements generally arise from:
- New statutory or regulatory mandates
- New threats
- New IT architecture initiatives with new stakeholders or requirements

7.2.1   Integrating with the ADM – Preliminary Phase

Within the Preliminary phase, the applicable regulatory and security policy requirements are defined and documents as part of defining the overall enterprise architecture. A written security policy must exist as well as a program for communicating and educating the organization. Typically, the requirements come from the policy and are applied to the architecture to be fulfilled.

Within the Preliminary phase, the security architect and team are identified. The first-order assumptions and boundary conditions are identifies, specifically to establish interfaces and protocols for exchanging security information related to identity, authentication, and authorization in federated systems.

The inputs of security in the Preliminary phase are:
- Written security policies
- Relevant statutes
- List of jurisdictions

The security outputs of the Preliminary Phase are:
- Applicable regulations
- Applicable security policies
- Security team roster
- Security assumptions and boundary conditions

7.2.2   Integrating with the ADM – Architecture Vision

The Architecture Vision phase focuses on the defining the relevant stakeholders and discovery of concerns and key business requirements related to security and the architecture. The activities of the phase related to security include:
- Obtaining management support for security measures
- Defining sign-off milestones of the architecture development cycle
- Determining and documenting applicable disaster recovery and business continuity requirements and plans
- Identifying and documenting the anticipated environment(s) where systems will be deployed
- Determining and documenting the system criticality

The security inputs of the Architecture Vision are:
- Applicable security policies
- Applicable jurisdictions
- Disaster recovery and business continuity plans

The security outputs of the Architecture Vision are:

- Physical security environment statements
- Business security environment statements
- Regulatory environment statements
- Security policy cover letter
- Architecture development checkpoints
- Applicable disaster recovery and business continuity plans
- Systems criticality statement

7.2.3 Integrating with the ADM – Business Architecture

The expectations related to security of the Business Architecture include:

- Determining the legitimate actors interacting with the product, service, or process in question
- Assessing the security-specific business processes for a baseline perspective
- Determining the burden of security measures on users and administrative personnel
- Identifying and documenting interconnecting systems
- Determining the assets at risk during a failure
- Identifying and documenting the ownership of assets
- Determining and documenting security forensic processes
- Identifying the criticality of the availability and correct operation of the service
- Determining and documenting the cost of security as it relates to the threats and value of the assets
- Reassessing and confirming Architecture Vision decisions
- Assessing alignment or conflict of identified security policies
- Performing threat analysis

The inputs of the Business Architecture related to security are:

- Business and regulatory security environment statements
- Applicable disaster recovery and business continuity plans
- Applicable security policies and regulations

The outputs of the Business Architecture are:

- Forensic processes

- New disaster recovery and business continuity requirements
- Validated business and regulatory environment statements
- Validated security policies and regulations
- Target security processes
- Baseline security processes
- Security actors
- Interconnecting systems
- Statement of security tolerance
- Asset list
- List of trust paths
- Availability impact statements
- Threat Analysis matrix

7.2.4 Integrating with the ADM – Information Systems Architecture

To support the security initiatives, the information Systems Architecture phase consists of several activities:

- Assessing the security-specific architecture elements for a baseline perspective
- Identifying safe default actions and failure states
- Identifying and evaluating applicable guidelines and standards
- Revisiting assumptions related to interconnecting systems
- Determining and documenting the sensitivity or classification level of information
- Identifying and documenting custody or assets
- Identifying the critical nature of the availability and operation of each function
- Determining the relationship of the system with business disaster and continuity plans
- Identifying the configurable aspect of the system to reflect security policies
- Identifying lifespan of used information
- Determine whether to mitigate, accept, transfer, or avoid identified risks
- Identifying actions and events that warrant logging or triggering

70

- Identifying and documenting requirements for accurate logging
- Identifying avenues of attack
- Performing threat analysis

The security inputs of the Information Systems Architecture phase are:

- Threat analysis matrix
- Risk analysis
- Documented forensic processes
- Validated business policies and regulation
- Interconnecting systems
- New disaster recovery and business continuity requirements

The security outputs of the Information Systems Architecture phase are:

- Event log-level matrix and requirements
- Risk management strategy
- Data lifecycle definitions
- Configurable system elements
- Baseline list of security-related elements
- New or augmented security-related elements
- Security use-case models
- Applicable security standards
- Validated interconnected system list
- Information classification report
- Asset custodians
- Function criticality statement
- Revised disaster recovery and business continuity plans
- Refined threat analysis matrix

7.2.5   Integrating with the ADM – Technology Architecture

Security related activities within the Technology Architecture phase of the ADM are:

- Assessing the security-specific architecture elements for a baseline perspective
- Revising assumptions about interconnecting systems
- Identifying and evaluating applicable guidelines and standards
- Identifying methods for regulating resource consumption
- Engineering a method for continuously measuring and communicating security measures
- Identifying the clearance level of users, administrators, and interconnecting systems
- Identifying minimal privileges required to achieve a technical or business objectives
- Identifying mitigating security measures
- Performing threat analysis

The security inputs to the Technology Architecture phase are:

- Security-related elements of a system
- Interconnected systems
- Applicable security standards
- Security actors
- Risk management strategy
- Validated security policies
- Validated regulatory requirements
- Validated business policies related to clearances

The security outputs of the Technology Architecture phase are:

- Baseline list of security technologies
- Validated interconnected systems list
- Selected security standards
- Resource conservation plan
- Security metrics and monitoring plan
- User authorization policies
- Risk management plan
- User clearance requirements

Copyright The Art of Service | Brisbane, Australia | Email:service@theartofservice.com
Web: http://theartofservice.com | eLearning: http://theartofservice.org | Phone: +61 (0)7 3252 2055

7.2.6 Integrating with the ADM – Opportunities and Solutions

The Opportunities and Solutions phase supports security concerns with the following activities:
- Identifying existing security services
- Engineering mitigation measures for identified risks
- Evaluating security software and security system resources
- Identifying new code, resources, and assets for re-use
- Performing threat analysis

7.2.7 Integrating with the ADM – Migration Planning

The Migration Planning phase support security through:
- Assessing the impact of new security measures on new and existing systems
- Implementing assurance methods
- Identifying secure installation parameters, initial conditions, and configurations
- Implementing disaster and business continuity plans
- Performing threat analysis

7.2.8 Integrating with the ADM – Implementation Governance

The Implementation Governance by addresses security concerns:
- Establishing reviews for architecture artifacts, design, and code and defining acceptance criteria
- Implementing methods and procedures to review evidence
- Performing threat analysis

7.3 Service Oriented Architectures

Business environments are becoming significantly more sophisticated. Service Oriented Architecture (SOA) as a concept provides an architectural style, which intends to simplify the business and its interoperability. When applied to software development, SOA structures applications in order to facilitate system flexibility and agility.

Service Oriented Architecture is becoming more present as a business opportunity to allow organizations to be structured to provide open, agile and flexible solutions. A business-led SOA approach has several fundamental aspects:
- Rich domain knowledge of horizontal and vertical concerns
- A structured, quantitative understanding of business value, costs, differentiations, and quality measures
- Broad understanding of current capability
- Broad understanding of the feasibility and viability of SOA technology-driven solutions

7.3.1 Business-Led and Developer-Led SOA

A business service is a unit of business capability supported by a combination of people, processes, and technology from the perspective of business-led SOA. Business services can be:
- Fulfilled by manual or automated processes
- Fulfilled within an organization of outsourced
- fulfilled at the point of use, a divisional level or as a corporate competency center
- Exposed to employees, customers, partners, or suppliers in any combination

A information system service is a unit of application code providing an open interface from the perspective of a developer-led SOA.

These services support a separation of concerns between:

- Process services as an encapsulation of business flow and application composition
- Application Services as an encapsulation of application function
- Data services as management of data access and persistence
- Infrastructure services as a commodity and sharing of common utility functions

Though business-led and developer-led SOA's have different focuses, their activities are complementary. The separation of service types aid in the specialization of infrastructure and tooling for the optimization of development, maintenance, and operational performance.

7.3.2 Issues with SOA

SOA is challenged by the alignment between business and IT within the organization. Adding services or breaking services into more granular business functions and application can increase complexity around the usage or and interaction between services, particularly:

- New stress points created around understanding relationships between technology and service portfolios
- New stress points created around SLA definition, governance, and impact management
- New stress points created around tracing business to IT
- New stress points created around communication, alignment, and semantics
- New stress points created around platform and interoperability
- New stress points created around performance visibility and optimization

Though technology can provide solutions to manage many of these stress points, the problem really understands the IT landscape as it applies to the business is required for effective operation of an SOA.

The problem is characterized by:
- "Service sprawl", or unplanned, misaligned services at inappropriate levels of granularity
- Inability to carry out assessment of impact resulting in overspending and poor service quality
- Multiple technology stacks which are costly and provide no interoperability
- Inability to identify services for re-use

7.3.3 Supporting SOA

Enterprise architecture applies architectural discipline to the end-to-end enterprise, treating the enterprise as a system. To assist SOA disciplines within the organization, enterprise architecture provides the following tools and techniques:
- Defined structured traceable representation of business and technology that link IT to the business
- Defined principles, constraints, frameworks, patterns, and standards which form the basis for design governance, ensuring aligned services, interoperability, and re-use
- Links different perspectives to a single business problem and establishing a consistent model to address various problem domains and test of completeness
- Provides consistent abstractions of strategies and project deliverables to allow bottom-up and top-down outputs to be compiled into a shared repository for planning and analysis

Enterprise architecture becomes a foundation for service oriented architecture by linking SOA stakeholders together, providing a link between business to IT, identifying services and their design for interoperability and a structured repository for information.

7.3.4   SOA and TOGAF

The concept s of SOA and TOGAF support each other, including:
- Function
- Business Service
- Information System Service
- Application Component
- Technology Component

7.3.5   Service Contract Definition

Service Contracts are used to define how different services interact. Some of the considerations of the service contract are:
- Service Governance
- Service Contracts
- Service Lifecycle Management
- Service Metadata

The service contract is used to communication and enforces policies, and ensures a healthy relationship between service providers and customers. The contract establishes agreement and enables trust to be maintained between parties.

A service contract can be either a governance contract between two business entities to define their interaction or an operational contract, which defines the actual communication protocols, and message formats. TOGAF is concerned with the governance contract.

7.4   Architecture Principles

Principles are general rules and guidelines intended for a long life to inform and support the direction the organization takes to fulfill its mission.

Principles can be established at one of all of the three levels of an organization:

- Enterprise principles support the decision-making performed throughout the enterprise.
- Information technology (IT) principles provide guidance on the use and deployment of all IT resources and assets int eh enterprise.
- Architecture principles are a subset of IT principles that relate to architecture work and either govern the architecture process or govern the implementation of the architecture.

7.4.1 Architecture Principles

Architecture principles define those rules and guidelines for using and deploying IT resources and asset. The principles reflect a consensus across the enterprise and provide a basis for decisions. The y should relate back to business objectives and key architecture drivers clearly.

7.4.2 Defining Principles

When defining principles, a standard way for defining them make sit easier to identify and utilize in the enterprise.

Each principle should follow the same format, which includes:

- Name – title representing the essence of the rule
- Statement – communicates the fundamental rule clearly and unambiguously
- Rationale – identifies the business benefits for adhering to the principle using business terminology
- Implication – highlights the business and IT requirements for carrying out the principle

7.4.3   Developing Principles

The lead enterprise architect with input from the enterprise CIO, Architecture Board, and key business stakeholders develops architecture principles. Each principle must have supporting policies and procedures to support their implementation.

Architecture principles are influenced in their development by:
- Enterprise mission and plans -
- Enterprise strategic initiatives
- External constraints such as market factors and legislation
- Current systems and technology
- Computer industry trends

Principles are considered good if they meet the following criteria:
- Understandable – quickly grasped and understood throughout the organization
- Robust – enabling quality decisions about architectures, plans, policies, and standards
- Complete – ensures that the principle is defined for every conceivable situation
- Consistent – allows a balance of interpretations in order to fulfill seemingly contradictory principles
- Stable – focuses on enduring principles that can accommodate change when required.

7.4.4   Applying Principles

Principles can be applied to the enterprise by:
- Providing a framework to make conscious decisions about IT
- Establishing relevant evaluation criteria
- Driving the definitions for functional requirements of the architecture
- Providing input to assess existing IS/IT systems and future strategic portfolios
- Highlight the value of the architecture specifically through the Rationale statements

- Providing an outline of the key tasks, resources, and potential costs specifically through the Implication statements
- Supporting architecture governance by providing a stake to allow interpretation in compliance assessments and supporting the decision to initiate a dispensation request

Principles are related to each other and are applied as a set. In some cases, one principle will take precedence over another principle to meet certain situations.

7.4.5 Common Principles

From the US Government's Federal Enterprise Architecture Framework, the following principles demonstrate their application across the business, data, application, and technology domains.

Business Principles:
Principle 1:   Primacy of Principles
Statement: Applies to all organizations with the enterprise.
Rationale: Adherence to principles provides a consistent and measurable level of quality information to decision-makers.
Implication: Information management initiatives will begin after being examined for compliance with the principles.

Principle 2:   Maximize Benefit to the Enterprise
Statement: Information management decisions provide maximum benefit to the enterprise.
Rationale: Decisions from an enterprise perspective have more long-term value than from any organizational perspective.
Implication: Some organizations will have to concede their own preferences for the greater benefit of the enterprise.

Principle 3:   Information Management in Everybody's Business
Statement: All organizations must be involved in information management decisions required to accomplish business objectives.
Rationale: Information users, as key stakeholders or customer, must be involved in any application of technology to address a business need.

Implication: Every stakeholder or customer must take responsibility for developing the information environment.

Principle 4:   Business Continuity
Statement: Enterprise operations must be maintained despite system failures.
Rationale: Hardware failure, natural disasters, and data corruption must not disrupt enterprise activities.
Implication: Recoverability, redundancy, and maintainability are issues to be addressed during design of systems.

Principle 5:   Common Use Applications
Statement: Applications should be developed for use across the enterprise is preferable over applications developed for use by a particular organization.
Rationale: Duplicate capability is expensive and encourages conflicting data.
Implication: Organizations will not be allowed to develop capabilities for their own use, which is similar to enterprise-wide capabilities.

Principle 6:   Service Orientation
Statement: Services within an architecture are designed to mirror real-world business activities.
Rationale: Service orientation delivers enterprise agility and Boundaryless Information Flow.
Implication: Business descriptions provide context for services while service orientation places unique requirements on the infrastructure.

Principle 7:   Compliance with Law
Statement: Enterprise information management processes comply with all relevant laws, policies, and regulations.
Rationale: Abiding by laws, policies, and regulations must be part of Enterprise policy.
Implication: The enterprise must have access to the rules, as well as education on compliance requirements.

Principle 8:   IT Responsibility
Statement: The IT organization is responsible for owning and implementing IT processes and information, which meet user-defined requirements for functionality, service levels, cost, and delivery timing.
Rationale: Solutions that are efficient and effective also have reasonable costs and clear benefits.
Implication: IT functions must define processes to manage business unit expectations.

Principle 9:   Protection of Intellectual Property
Statement: The protection of the enterprise's Intellectual Property must be reflected in the IT architecture, implementation and governance processes.
Rationale: An enterprise's Intellectual Property is hosted in the IT domain.
Implication: A security policy, which governs human and IT actors, is required to substantially improve protection of IP.

Data Principles:
Principle 10:   Data is an Asset
Statement: Data, as an asset, has value to the enterprise and must be managed accordingly.
Rationale: Data aids decision-making, making it a valuable corporate resource that must be appropriately managed.
Implication: Data stewards must have the authority and means to manage data in order to prevent obsolete, incorrect, or inconsistent data from being proliferated int eh enterprise.

Principle 11:   Data is shared
Statement: Users must have access to shared data necessary to perform their duties.
Rationale: IT is less expensive to maintain accurate data in a single application and share it, instead of maintaining duplicate data in multiple applications.
Implication: Enabling data sharing requires that policies, procedures, and standards governing data management and access must be developed and used. Data sharing will require a massive change in culture.

Principle 12:   Data is Accessible
Statement: Data must be accessible to users to enable their performance of duties.
Rationale: Efficiency and effectiveness in decision-making is enabled by the wide access to data from the enterprise.
Implication: The ease that users can obtain information is a function of accessibility.

Principle 13:   Data Trustee
Statement: Data elements must have a trustee accountable for data quality.
Rationale: Trustees must have sole responsibility for data entry to eliminate redundant human effort and data storage resources.
Implication: Data trustees will be responsible for meeting quality requirements on the data they are accountable.

Principle 14:   Common Vocabulary and Data Definitions
Statement: Definitions that are understandable and available to all users are consistently given to data.
Rationale: A common vocabulary facilitates communications and enable effective dialog throughout the enterprise.
Implication: Initial common vocabulary must be established in the enterprise. Definition will be used uniformly and new data definitions must be defined in cooperation and reconcile with other definitions.

Principle 15:   Data Security
Statement: Data is protected from unauthorized use and disclosure.
Rationale: A balance must be made between security and privacy of data and free and open access.
Implication: To provide access to open information while maintaining a secure environment, security must be a concern at the data level, not the application.

Application Principles:
Principle 16:   Technology Independence
Statement: Applications can operate on multiple technology patterns when independent of specific technology choices.
Rationale: Independence of applications from the technology allows applications to be developed, upgraded, and operated cost-effectively and timely.

Implication: Standards supporting portability must be in place.

Principle 17: Ease-of-Use
Statement: Applications must be easy to use and the technology transparent to users.
Rationale: Ease-of-use encourages users to work inside an integrated information environment.
Implication: Applications will require having a common look and feel.

Technology Principles:
Principle 18: Requirements-Based Change
Statement: Change to applications and technology are made in response to business needs.
Rationale: Unintended effects on business due to IT changes ill are minimized.
Implication: Change management processes to support these principles must be developed and implemented.

Principle 19: Responsive Change Management
Statement: Changes to the enterprise are implemented in a timely manner.
Rationale: The information environment must be responsive to the users needs.
Implication: Processes for managing and implementing change must be developed to prevent delays in execution.

Principle 20: Control Technical Diversity
Statement: Control of technology diversity minimizes the non-trivial cost of maintaining expertise of multiple processing environments.
Rationale: Limiting the number of supported technological components will simplify maintainability and reduce costs.
Implication: Policies, standards, and procedures that govern acquisition of technology must control the diversity of that technology.

Stakeholder management provides a discipline for gaining support between architecture practitioners and benefits the enterprise by:

- Identifying powerful stakeholders early for their input to shape the architecture.
- Obtaining support from powerful stakeholders to enable more resources to be available during engagement of architectures.
- Early and frequent communications with stakeholders allow better understanding of the architecture process.
- Reaction to architecture models and reports can be more effectively anticipated.

Stakeholder analysis is used in the Architecture Vision phase to identify the key players in the engagement and updated with each subsequent phase of the ADM. The complexity of architecture can be difficult to manage and obtain agreement from large numbers of stakeholders. TOGAF addresses these issues throughout the ADM using the concepts of:

- Stakeholders
- Concerns
- Views
- Viewpoints

7.5.1 Stakeholder Management Process

The process for stakeholder management includes the following steps:

- Identify Stakeholders – typically includes senior executives, project organization roles, client organization roles, system developers, alliance partners, suppliers, IT operations, and customers impacted by the enterprise architecture project.
- Classify Stakeholder Positions – analyzing the stakeholders to determine their readiness to support the effort.

85

- Determine Stakeholder Management Approach – identifies the direction of the enterprise architecture effort to engage with the stakeholders that have the greatest power or interest to successfully support the effort.
- Tailor Engagement Deliverables – Identify the viewpoints, matrices, and views that need to be produced to support demonstrating the enterprise architecture's ability to address a particular stakeholder's concerns.

7.6 Architecture Patterns

A pattern is a reusable object that was useful in one practical situation and has the potential to be useful in other similar situations. Formalizing the process to capture patterns is beneficial for an organization as a way to acknowledge, build, and share best practices in support.

Patterns provide an opportunity to architects to identify combinations of Architecture and Solution Building Blocks.

7.6.1 Pattern Content

The content of a pattern contains:
- Name – unique heading reference for the pattern
- Problem – description of the situation where pattern is applied
- Context – the existing preconditions where the pattern is applicable
- Forces – description of the relevant forces and constraints
- Solution – description of pattern details
- Resulting Context – the post-conditions present after applying the pattern
- Examples – sample applications of the pattern
- Rationale – a explanation of the pattern
- Related Problems – a description of any relationships between this pattern and other patterns
- Known Uses – known applications of the pattern in the existing systems

7.6.2   Terminology of Patterns

- Architecture Pattern – a fundamental structural organization or schema providing a set of predefined subsystems, responsibilities, and rules and guidelines.
- Design Pattern – a scheme for refining the subsystems or components of a system and their relationships.
- Idiom – a low-level pattern describing how particulate aspects of components are implemented.
- Architecture Continuum – provides a repository for relevant re-usable architecture patterns to be used within Phases A through D of the ADM.
- Views – patterns assist in designing models that represent a complete system architecture and composing views based on those models.
- Business Scenarios – patterns may be identified in business scenarios.

7.7   Business Scenarios

Business Scenarios are used at various stages of the enterprise architecture to assist in identifying and understanding business needs and linking business requirements to the enterprise architecture.

A business scenario will describe:
- Business processes, applications , or set of applications enabled by the architecture
- Business and technology environment
- People and computing components executing the scenario
- Desired outcomes from proper execution

Used to represent a significant business need or problem and enabling vendors to understand the value of the architectural solution, business scenarios are 'SMART':
- Specific – defining what needs to be done
- Measurable – providing clear measures of success
- Actionable – determining the elements and plans for the solution

- Realistic – solving the problem within the physical reality, time, and cost constraints
- Time-bound – clearly stating the expiration of the solution opportunity

7.7.1 Benefits to Business Scenarios

The benefit of a business scenario ensures:
- The set of requirements addressed by the business scenario can be confirmed accurate and lead to better development of the architecture.
- The business value for solving the problem is clear.
- The relevancy of potential solutions can be determined clearly.

A business scenario is a complete description of a business problem enabling individual requirements to be reviewed in relationship to the context of the overall problem.

7.7.2 Business Scenario Process

Creating a business scenario involves:
- Identifying, documenting, and ranking problems driving the scenario.
- Identifying the business and technical environment of the scenario and documenting in scenario models.
- Identifying and documenting desired objectives.
- Identifying the human actors and their role in the business model.
- Identifying computer actors and their role in the business model.
- Identifying and documenting roles, responsibilities, and measures of success.
- Checking for 'fitness-for-purpose.'

The development of business scenarios involve several iterative phases of gathering, analyzing, and reviewing information contained in the business scenario.

The Gathering phase focuses on collecting information in each of the steps of the process. The techniques used to collect range form information research and surveying to quantitative and qualitative analysis.

The analyzing phase processes and documents the gathered information and models are created to represent the information. Linkages between key elements of the business scenario are maintained using matrices related to business processes and its:

- Constituencies
- Human and Computer Actors
- Issues
- Objectives

The Reviewing phase feed back the results of analysis to the sponsors to gain shared understanding of the problem and the depth of impact.

7.7.3 Business Scenarios Contents

Documentation of business scenarios contains all-important details about the scenario. Content types are either graphical (models) or descriptive text; many case both.

Models capture business and technology views in a graphical form to enable comprehension. Descriptions capture details in textual form.

7.7.4 Goals and Objectives

The overall goals and objectives for developing architecture are mapped to business goals and objectives and provide guidance in developing business scenarios and solutions. Goals and objectives are SMART.

Below is a list of goals and generic objectives:

Improve Business Process Performance
- Increased process throughput
- Consistent output quality

89

- Predictable process costs
- Increased re-use of existing processes
- Reduced time of sending business information

Decrease Costs
- Redundancies and duplication at lower levels of enterprise assets
- Decreased reliance on external service providers
- Lower costs of maintenance

Improve Business Operations
- Increased budget
- Decreased costs
- Decreased time-to-market
- Increased quality of services
- Improve quality of business information

Improve Management Efficiency
- Increased business flexibility
- Shorter decision making time
- Higher quality decisions

Reduce Risk
- Ease of implementation
- Decreased errors from complex and faulty systems
- Decreased real-world safety hazards

Improve Effectiveness of IT Organization
- Increases rollout of new projects
- Decreased time to rollout
- Lower cost in rolling out new projects
- Decreased loss of service continuity during roll-out
- Common development
- Open system environment
- Use of off-the-shelf products
- Software re-use
- Resource sharing

Improve User Productivity
- Consistent user interface
- Integrated applications
- Data sharing

Improve Portability and Scalability
- Portability
- Scalability

Improve Interoperability
- Common infrastructure
- Standardization

Increase Vendor Independence
- Interchangable components
- Non-proprietary specifications

Reduce Lifecycle Costs
- Reduced duplication
- Reduced software maintenance costs
- Incremental replacement
- Reduced training costs

Improve Security
- Consistent security interfaces for applications
- Consistent security interfaces for users
- Security independence

Improve Manageability
- Consistent management interface
- Reduced operation, administration, and maintenance costs

7.8 Gap Analysis

To validate a developing architecture, gap analysis is used throughout the Architecture Development Method.

The potential sources of gaps include:
- Business Domain
  - People
  - Process
  - Tools
  - Information
  - Measurement
  - Financial
  - Facilities
- Data Domain
  - Insufficient currency
  - Missing data
  - Wrong data
  - Data availability
  - Data not created
  - Data not used
  - Data relationships
- Application domain
  - Impacted applications
  - Eliminated applications
  - Created applications
- Technology domain
  - Impacted technologies
  - Eliminated technologies
  - Created technologies

7.9 Migration Planning Techniques

7.9.1 Implementation Factor Assessment and Deduction Matrix

The factors influencing the Implementation and Migration Plan can be documented within the Implementation Factor Assessment and Deduction Matrix. The matrix includes each factor, a description of the factor, and the logical deductions indicating actions or constraints for consideration when creating the plan.

7.9.2 Consolidated Gaps, Solutions and Dependencies Matrix

When creating work packages, the Consolidated Gaps, Solutions, and Dependencies Matrix can be used as a planning tool. The purpose of the matrix is to view the architectures, group the gaps between the baseline and the target, the potential solutions and any dependencies in a convenient manner.

7.9.3 Architecture Definition Increments Table

To plan a series of Transition Architecture, an Architecture Definition Increments Table can be created. The table lists all the projects and allows the incremental deliverables to be assigned across the Transition Architectures.

7.9.4 Enterprise Architecture State Evolution Table

The Enterprise Architecture State Evolution Table can be used in conjunction with the Technical Reference Model (TRM) to show the proposed state of any architecture at various levels. Solution Building Blocks are described based on their delivery and impact on services from the TRM and marked to show progression of the enterprise architecture.

7.9.5 Business Value Assessment Technique

Business value is assessed by creating a matrix of the value index dimension and risk value dimension. The value index includes criteria for compliance to principles, financial contribution, strategic alignment, and competitive position. The risk index includes criteria for size, complexity, technology, organizational capacity, and impact of a failure. Each project is located within the matrix to allow for better decision-making related to all projects.

Copyright The Art of Service | Brisbane, Australia | Email:service@theartofservice.com
Web: http://theartofservice.com | eLearning: http://theartofservice.org | Phone: +61 (0)7 3252 2055

7.10.1 Defining Interoperability

Interoperability is categorized often in the following classes:
- Operational or Business Interoperability – defines the sharing behaviors for business processes
- Information Interoperability – defines the sharing behaviors for information
- Technical Interoperability – defines the sharing behaviors for technical services

The Enterprise Application Integration (EAI) defines interoperability in terms of:
- Presentation Integration/Interoperability – provides a common look and feel approach
- Information Integration/Interoperability – corporate information is seamlessly shared between corporate applications to obtain a common set of client information
- Application Integration/Interoperability – corporate functionality is integrated and shared to prevent duplicate applications
- Technical Integration/Interoperability – common methods and shared services for the communication, storage, processing, and access to data in the application platform and communications infrastructure domain

7.10.2 Enterprise Operating Model

Establishing interoperability requires a corporate operating model to be determined. An operating model provides a description for how an organization wants to thrive and grow. Complex enterprises can have more than one type of operating model.

7.10.3 Refining Interoperability

To implement interoperability requires the creation, management, acceptance, and enforcement of standards. The architecture is key for identifying standards. Interoperability should be refined to meet the needs of the enterprise. This refinement can be tracked through degrees:

- Degree 1: Unstructured Data Exchange – focuses on the exchange of human-interpretable unstructured data
- Degree 2: Structured Data Exchange – focuses on the exchange of human -interpretable structured data used for manual and/or automatic handling
- Degree 3: Seamless Sharing of Data – focuses on the automatic sharing of data based on a common exchange model
- Degree 4: Seamless Sharing of Information – focuses on the automatic sharing of universal interpretation of information

7.11 Business Transformation Readiness Assessment

The Business Transformation Readiness Assessment is used to evaluate and quantify an organization's readiness to undergo change.

The recommended activities to assess the readiness include:

- Determine the readiness factors that impact the organization
- use maturity models to present readiness factors
- Assess the readiness factors
- Assess the risks for each readiness factor
- Identify improvement actions to mitigate risk
- Work improvement actions into Implementation and Migration Plan

7.11.1 Determining Readiness Factors

In cooperation with individuals from different parts of the organization, factors affecting the business transformation association with the migration from baseline to target architectures should be identified

The Business Transformation Enablement Program (BTEP) for the Canadian Government recognizes the following factors:
- Vision – the ability to define and communicate achievements
- Desire – the desire to achieve results
- Willingness – the ability to accept the impact of doing the work required
- Resolve – the ability to complete the work effort
- Need – the underlying requirement for doing the work
- Business Case – creates a strong focus for the project
- Funding – a clear source of fiscal resources
- Sponsorship – establishes accountability
- Leadership – ensures everyone participates and focuses on the strategic goals
- Governance – the ability to engage the information and support of all portion to ensure corporate interests are served and their objectives achieved
- Accountability – the assignment of specific and appropriate responsibility
- Workable Approach and Execution Model – describes a clear executable steps in model form
- IT Capacity to Execute – the ability to perform all IT tasks required by a project
- Enterprise Capacity to Execute – the ability to perform all tasks required by an effort outside of the IT organization
- Enterprise Ability to Implement and Operate – a picture of the transformation elements and related business process and their ability to embrace change

7.11.2 Maturity Models

One method of presentation an organization's readiness is through maturity models. Each factor is converted into a model with a standard worksheet containing all the information and deductions required to determine the maturity.

The maturity model should enable:
- The Baseline Architecture maturity level to be assessed
- The target maturity level required to achieve the Target Architecture can be determined
- Intermediate targets to be achieved in a short time can be determined

7.11.3 Assessing Readiness

An assessment of readiness should address:
- Vision – determine where the enterprise has to evolve
- Rating – determines the importance of each factor with respect to urgency, readiness status, and degree of difficulty to fix
- Risks and Actions – defines the list of actions required for the factor to change to a favorable state

7.12 Risk Management

There are two levels of risk involved when implementing an architecture projects:
- Initial Level of Risk
- Residual Level of Risk

The process for risk management involves
- Risk classification
- Risk identification
- Initial risk assessment
- Risk mitigation and residual risk assessments
- Risk monitoring

97

7.12.1 Risk Classification

Classification of risk related to impact on the organization allows specific impacts to be addressed by different levels of governance. Different classifications include:
- Schedule (time)
- Budget (cost)
- Scope
- Client transformation relationship
- Contractual
- Technological
- Complexity
- Environmental or corporate
- Personnel
- Client acceptance

Classification allows risk management to be delegated appropriately.

7.12.2 Risk Identification

Risks can be identified through several avenues including;
- Any phase of the ADM
- Maturity assessments
- Transformation readiness assessments

Typically, risks can be discovered when considering the impact of not achieving targets or completing project.

7.12.3 Initial Risk Assessments

Measuring the effect and frequency of risks has no set rules. Best practices of risk management provide the following criteria to be used in assessments.

For Effect:
- Catastrophic – critical financial loss that has the possibility of bankruptcy

- Critical – serious financial loss in more than one line of business with a loss in productivity
- Marginal – financial loss in a single line of business and a reduced return on IT investment
- Negligible – minimal impact on a single line of business affecting their ability to deliver services or products

For Frequency:
- Frequent – likely to occur often or continuously
- Likely – occurs several times during a transformation cycle
- Occasional – occurs sporadically
- Seldom – remotely possible to occur
- Unlikely – Will not occur

Combining the criteria, corporate impact can be determined for risk:
- Extremely High Risk – most likely with fail with severe consequences
- High Risk – significant failure impacting in certain goals not being met
- Moderate Risk – noticeable failure threatening the success of certain goals
- Low Risk – Certain goals will not be successful

7.12.4 Residual Risk Assessments

Risk mitigation involves the identification, planning, and conduct of actions aimed at reducing risk to an acceptable level. The effort to mitigate risk can range from simple monitoring to the development of a complete contingency plan.

Residual risk assessment is conducted after mitigation steps are taken to determine the impact of the risk on the enterprise. To conduct the risk assessment, the effect and frequency is reassessed and the impact is recalculated.

Residual risk should be approved by the IT governance framework and be monitored to ensure that the enterprise is managing the residual risk and not the initial risk.

Copyright The Art of Service | Brisbane, Australia | Email:service@theartofservice.com
Web: http://theartofservice.com | eLearning: http://theartofservice.org | Phone: +61 (0)7 3252 2055

8 Architecture Content Framework

The Architecture Content Framework allows the TOGAF to be a stand-alone framework for architecture in an enterprise. It uses three categories to describe the type of architectural work product:

- Deliverable – a work product, which is contractually specified and formally reviewed, agreed, and signed off by the stakeholders. They typically represent outputs from projects.
- Artifact – a granular architecture work product describing architecture from a specific viewpoint.
- Building Block – a re-usable component of business, IT, or architectural capability that can be combined with other building blocks to deliver solutions and architectures.

8.1 Content Metamodel

All types of building blocks that may exist within architecture are defined in the content metamodel. Within the definition, the building blocks are described as will as their relationships with each other.

8.1.1 Content Metamodel Concepts

The core content metamodel concepts include:

- Core and extension content
- Formal and information modeling
- Core metamodel entities
- Catalog, matrix, and diagram concepts

The core and extension content is an introduction to how TOGAF employs a basic core metamodel and applies a number of extension modules to address specific issues in the architecture. It provides a minimum set of architectural content to support traceability across artifacts.

Extension modules are optional and selected during the Preliminary phase to meet the needs of the organization.

The extension modules found in the TOGAF Content Metamodel are:
- Governance Extensions
- Services Extensions
- Process Modeling Extensions
- Data Extensions
- Infrastructure Consolidation Extensions
- Motivation Extensions

8.1.2   Core Metamodel Entities

Core metamodel entities have some key relationship concepts:
- Processes should normally be used to describe flow
- Functions describe units of business capability
- Business services support organizational objectives and are defined at a level of granularity consistent with the level of governance needed
- Business services are deployed onto application components
- Application components are deployed onto technology components

Entities are used by the content metamodel to define how architectural concepts are captured, stored, filtered, queried, and represented in support consistency, completeness, and traceability in the architecture. General classes of entities include:
- Architecture Principles, Vision, and Requirements artifacts
- Business Architecture artifacts
- Information System Architecture artifacts
- Technology Architecture artifacts
- Architecture Realization artifacts

8.1.3   Catalog, Matrix, and Diagram Concept

Architectural information can be structured in an orderly way by the content metamodel. This allows the information to be processed to meet stakeholder needs effectively. To present the metamodel clearly to the stakeholders, catalogs, matrices, and diagrams are used.

Catalogs are lists of building blocks of a specific or related type for use as a reference or for governance. The metamodel can perform queries and analysis on the information.

Matrices show relationships between two or more model entities. They are displayed in grid format.

Diagrams render architectural content graphically to allow stakeholders to retrieve required information.

8.1.4   Core Architecture Artifacts

Each phase of the ADM contributes one or more artifacts to the core content metamodel:
- Preliminary
  - Principles Catalog
- Architecture Vision
  - Stakeholder Map Matrix
  - Value Chain Diagram
  - Solution Concept Diagram
- Business Architecture
  - Organization/Actor Catalog
  - Role Catalog
  - Business Service/Function Catalog
  - Business Interaction Matrix
  - Actor/Role Matrix
  - Business Footprint Diagram
  - Business Service/Information Diagram
  - Functional Decomposition Diagram
  - Product Lifecycle Diagram
- Information Systems (Data Architecture)
  - Data Entity/Data Component Catalog
  - Data Entity/Business Function Matrix
  - System/Data Matrix
  - Class Diagram
  - Data Dissemination Diagram

- Information Systems (Application Architecture)
  - Application Portfolio Catalog
  - Interface Catalog
  - System/Organization Matrix
  - Role/System Matrix
  - System/Function Matrix
  - Application Interaction Matrix
  - Application Communication Diagram
  - Application and User Location Diagram
  - System Use-case Diagram
- Technology Architecture
  - Technology Standards Catalog
  - Technology Portfolio Catalog
  - System/Technology Matrix
  - Environments and Locations Diagram
  - Platform Decomposition Diagram
- Opportunities and Solutions
  - Project Context Diagram
  - Benefits Diagram
- Requirements Management
  - Requirements Catalog

8.1.5   Content Metamodel Extensions

Governance Extensions serve to allow additional structured data to be held against objectives and business services. The extensions scope consists of the abilities to apply measures to objectives, to apply contracts to service communication or interactions, and to define reusable service qualities. The governance extension will also create diagrams to show ownership and management of systems. These extensions are useful when an organization is considering IT change and has granular requirements for service levels that differ between multiple services, or when an organization is looking to change its operational governance practices and has a strong focus on business drivers, goals, and objectives.

Services Extensions create a concept of IS services with business services to provide a sophisticated model of the service portfolio. IS services are supported by applications and create a layer of abstraction to ease the impact of constraints on business services.

Copyright The Art of Service | Brisbane, Australia | Email:service@theartofservice.com
Web: http://theartofservice.com | eLearning: http://theartofservice.org | Phone: +61 (0)7 3252 2055

Service extensions are used when a preset definition of services is in place but does not align to technical or architectural needs, or a different language is used by business and IT to describe similar capabilities, IT services do not align with business need, or IT is taking initial steps to engage business about IT architectures.

Process Modeling Extensions provide a detail model of process flows with events, products, and controls added to the metamodel. The extension is useful when the architecture must be mindful of the state and events, the architecture is required to identify and store process control steps and critical or elaborate process flows exist.

Data Extensions allow sophisticated data modeling and encapsulation of data. The scope of a data extension includes the creation of logical data components to group data entities, physical data components that implement logical data components, and data lifecycle, security, and mitigation diagrams of the architecture. Data extensions are found when architecture features are significantly complex and risky around location, encapsulation, and management of data access.

Infrastructure Consolidation Extensions are useful when the application and technology portfolios are fragmented and business as usual capability must be consolidated into a smaller number of components. The extension consists of crating location entities, logical and physical application components, and diagrams focusing on the location of assets, compliance with standards, and structure of applications, application migration, and infrastructure configuration. The extension may be present where duplicate or overlapping capability or functionality exists or application consolidation is required or planned.

Motivation Extensions provide structured modeling to drivers, goals, and objectives influencing an organization and showing their relationship to each other. The extension is useful when the architecture must understand the organizational motivation; drivers, goals, or objectives are in conflict with each other; or service levels are unknown or unclear.

8.2 Architectural Artifacts

To describe a system, solution, or state of the enterprise, architectural artifacts are created. Artifacts are essentially views into the architecture.

8.2.1 Basic Architecture Concepts

- Systems – a collection of components combined to accomplish a specific function of set of functions.
- Architecture – the fundamental organization of a system with its components, relationships and principles.
- Architecture Description – a collection of artifacts documenting architecture.
- Stakeholders – people with key roles or concerns with the system.
- Concerns – key interests important to the stakeholders of a of system and provide the acceptability criteria for a system.
- View – a representation of the system from a perspective of a set of concerns.
- Viewpoint – the perspective from which a view is taken.

A view is what is seen while a viewpoint is where the view originates. Where viewpoints are generic, and reusable, views are specific to the architecture it addresses.

8.2.2 Developing Views

Architecture views are developed through an iterative process, typically through the domains from business to technology and using business scenarios as the vehicle. The view should be usable within the current and target environments

The process for creating views includes:
- Refer to an existing library viewpoints
- Select the appropriate viewpoints based on stakeholders and concerns

- Generate views using the selected viewpoints as templates

8.2.3 Viewpoints

Viewpoints are found in three classes:
- Catalogs – represent lists of building blocks
- Matrices – show relationships between building blocks
- Diagrams – graphical viewpoints presenting building blocks

Viewpoints within TOGAF architecture domains group the different classes and focus a specific set of people:
- Business Architecture – supports users, planners, and business management
- Data Architecture – supports database designers, database administrators, and system engineers
- Application Architecture – supports system and software engineers
- Technology Architecture – supports acquirers, operators, administrators, and managers

8.3 Architecture Deliverables

The TOGAF Content Frameworks recognizes deliverables that are produced as outputs from executing the ADM cycle. Deliverables may be produced elsewhere and consumed within the ADM.

Below are a listing of architecture deliverables and their contents.

8.3.1 Architecture Contract

Joint agreements between development partners and sponsors on the deliverables, quality, and fitness-for-purpose of an architecture.

Contents of an Architecture Design and Development Contract:

- Architecture and strategic principles and requirements
- Conformance requirements
- Architecture development and management process and roles
- Target Architecture measures
- Defined phases of deliverables
- Prioritized joint workplan
- Time window(s)
- Architecture delivery and business metrics

Contents of a Business Users' Architecture Contract:
- Introduction and background
- The nature of the agreement
- Scope of the architecture
- Strategic requirements
- Conformance requirements
- Architecture adopters
- Time Windows(s)
- Architecture business metrics
- Service architecture and SLAs

8.3.2   Architecture Definition Document

A deliverable container for the core architectural artifacts created during a project. The Architecture Definition Document is a companion document to the Architecture Requirements Specification.

The content s of the Architecture Definition document is:
- Scope
- Goals, objectives, and constraints
- Architecture principles
- Baseline Architecture
- Architecture models
- Rationale and justification for approach
- Mapping to Architecture Repository
- Gap analysis
- Impact Assessment

8.3.3 Architecture Principles

General rules and guidelines to inform and support how an organization fulfills its mission

8.3.4 Architecture Repository

A storage area for all architecture-related projects within the enterprise.

The content of the Architecture Repository include:
- Architecture Frameworks
- Standards Information Base
- Architecture Landscape
- Reference Architectures
- Governance Log

8.3.5 Architecture Requirements Specification

A set of quantitative statements, which outline what actions, an implementation project must take on to comply with the architecture.

The contents of the Architecture Requirements Specification include:
- Success measures
- Architecture requirements
- Business service contracts
- Application service contracts
- Implementation guidelines
- Implementation specifications
- Implementation standards
- Implementation requirements
- Constraints
- Assumptions

8.3.6 Architecture Roadmap

A listing of individual increments of change and shows the progression from Baseline Architecture to the Target Architecture.

The contents of the Architecture Roadmap include:
- Project list
- Time-oriented Migration Plan
- Implementation recommendations

8.3.7 Architecture Vision

A high-level view of the final architecture product.

The content of the Architecture Vision includes:
- Problem description
- Detailed objectives
- Environment and process models
- Actors and their roles and responsibilities
- Resulting architecture model

8.3.8 Capability Assessment

Provides an understanding of the baseline and target capability level of the enterprise.

The contents of the Capability Assessment are:
- Business Capability Assessment
- IT Capability Assessment
- Architecture Maturity Assessment
- Business Transformation Readiness Assessment

8.3.9   Change Request

Formalized attempt to request a change to the architecture.

The content of a Change Request includes:
- Description of the proposed change
- Rationale for the proposed change
- impact assessment of the proposed change
- Repository reference number

8.3.10 Communications Plan

Provides a basis for communicating within a planned and managed process to stakeholders.

The contents of a Communication Plan include:
- Identification of stakeholders and grouping by communication requirements
- Identification of communication needs,
- Identification of communication mechanisms
- Identification of a communications timetable

8.3.11 Compliance Assessment

Provides a basis for determining and documenting compliance to the architecture.

The contents of the Compliance Assessment are:
- Overview of project progress and status
- Overview of project architecture and design
- Completed architecture checklists

8.3.12 Implementation and Migration Plan

A schedule for implementation of the Transition Architecture solution:
- Implementation and Migration Strategy
- Interactions with other management frameworks
- Project charters
- Implementation Plan

8.3.13 Implementation Governance Model

Enables Transition Architectures to be governed while being implemented into the enterprise.

The contents of the Implementation Governance Model include:
- Governance processes
- Governance organization structure
- Governance roles and responsibilities
- Governance checkpoints and criteria for success

8.3.14 Organizational Model for Enterprise Architecture

Demonstrates the organization, roles and responsibility within the enterprise.

The content of the Organizational Model for Enterprise Architecture consists of:
- Scope of organizations impacted
- Maturity assessment, gaps, and resolution approach
- Roles and responsibilities for architecture team(s)
- Constraints on architecture work
- Budget requirements
- Governance and support strategy

8.3.15 Request for Architecture Work

Sent from sponsoring organizations to the architecture organization to trigger the start of an architecture development cycle.

The contents of a Request for Architecture Work consist of:
- Organization sponsors
- Organization's mission statement
- Business goals (and changes)
- Strategic plans of the business
- Time limits
- Changes in the business environment
- Organizational constraints
- Budget information and financial constraints
- External constraints and business constraints
- Current business system description
- Current architecture and IT system description
- Description of developing organization
- Description of resources available to developing organization

8.3.16 Requirements Impact Assessment

Assesses the current architecture requirements and specification to identify changes to be made and the implications of those changes.

The contents of the Requirements Impact Assessment consist of:
- Reference to specific requirements
- Stakeholder priority of the requirements to date
- Phases to be revisited
- Phase to lead on requirements prioritization
- Results of phase investigations and revised priorities
- Recommendations on management of requirements
- Repository reference number

8.3.17 Statement of Architecture Work

Defines the scope and approach used to complete an architecture project.

The contents of a Statement of Architecture Work are:
- Statement of Architecture Work title
- Project request and background
- Project description and scope
- Overview of Architecture Vision
- Managerial approach
- Change of scope procedures
- Roles, responsibilities, and deliverables
- Acceptance criteria and procedures
- Project plan and schedule
- Support of the Enterprise Continuum
- Signature approvals

8.3.18 Tailored Architecture Framework

Adopting the industry standard TOGAF for integration into en enterprise.

The content of the Tailored Architecture Framework includes:
- Tailored architecture method
- Tailored architecture content
- Configured and deployed tools
- Interfaces with governance models and other frameworks

8.3.19 Transition Architecture

Demonstrates the enterprise at incremental states reflecting periods of transition between the Baseline and Transition Architectures.

The contents of the Transition Architecture are:
- Opportunity portfolio
- Work package portfolio
- Milestones
- Implementation Factor Assessment and Deduction Matrix
- Consolidated Gaps, Solutions, and Dependencies Matrix

8.4 Building Blocks

The characteristics of building blocks are:
- They are a package of functionality defined to meet business need.
- They have a type corresponding to the TOGAF content metamodel.
- They have a defined boundary and are recognized as an entity by domain experts.
- They interoperate with other inter-dependent building blocks.
- Well-crafted building blocks consider implementation, usage, evolves to exploit technology and standards, may be assembled from other building blocks or be used to assemble other building blocks, and be re-usable and replaceable.

Systems are built using collections of building blocks. Two types of building blocks can be used: Architecture Building Blocks (ABB) and Solution Building Blocks (SBB).

8.4.1 Architecture Building Blocks

Architecture Building Blocks (ABBs) are related to the Architecture Continuum. They are defined and selected because of the application of the ADM.

ABBs capture architecture requirements and direct and guide the development of solution Building Blocks.

At a minimum, ABBs must have the following specifications:
- Fundamental functionality and attributes
- Interfaces
- Interoperability and relationship to other building blocks
- Dependent building blocks contain required functionality and named user interfaces
- Map to business and organizational entities and policies

8.4.2 Solution Building Blocks

Solution Building Blocks (SBBs) are related to the Solutions Continuum. They are developed or procured.

SBBs define what products and components will implement the functionality and their implementation. They fulfill business requirements using products of services for vendors.

At a minimum, SBBs must have:
- Specific functionality and attributes
- Interfaces
- Required SBBs contain required functionality and named user interfaces
- Mapping from the SBBs to the IT topology and operational policies
- Specifications of attributes
- Performance
- Configurability
- Design drivers and constraints
- Relationships between SBBs and ABBs

115

9   Enterprise Continuum

The Enterprise Continuum provides a view of the Architecture Repository, which has methods for classifying architecture and solution artifacts. The artifacts can be external or internal to the Architecture Repository and evolve. The Enterprise Continuum is useful to promote communication and understanding between individual enterprises, as well as with vendors and customers. It also allows clearer organization of re-usable architecture and solution assets

9.1   Basic Concepts

As a view of all the architecture assets within the repository, the Enterprise Continuum can contain architecture descriptions, models, building blocks, patterns, viewpoints, and other artifacts. These artifacts are in place because the enterprise considers them available for the development of architectures.

9.1.1   Components of Enterprise Continuum

The Enterprise Continuum is organized into three distinct partitions:
- Enterprise Continuum – the outermost continuum, which classifies assets, related to the context of the overall enterprise architecture. The classes of assets may influence the developing architectures, but are not directly used in the development. Two specialization areas are found within this continuum: Architecture Continuum and Solution continuum.
- Architecture Continuum – consistently defines and communicates the generic rules, representations, and relationships in architecture. Within the continuum, Architecture Building Blocks (ABBs) are structured as re-usable assets. The continuum provides a basis for evolving ABBS from generic entities to fully expressed assets, which are specific to the organization.

- Solution Continuum – consistently describes and communicates the implementation of assets defined in the Architecture Continuum. Solution Building Blocks (SBBs) are the primary content of the Continuum and represent the results of implemented rules and relationships defined in the architecture continuum as a product of agreements between t he customer and business partners.

9.1.2   Enterprise Continuum

Assets, which are available to an enterprise, are classified and reside within the Enterprise Continuum. TOGAF is a framework for developing and managing enterprise architecture for a specific organization. Not all assets within the Enterprise Continuum will be considered for a TOGAF framework. Despite this, the currency and accuracy of the Enterprise Continuum is paramount for the success for the TOGAF framework.

Architectures will identify and incorporate specific contextual factors, including:
- External influencing factors, such as regulatory change, advances in technology, and competitiveness
- Business strategy and context, such as mergers, acquisitions, and other transformational requirements
- Current business operations

9.1.3   Architecture Continuum

Howe architectures develop and evolve across a continuum can be demonstrated through the Architecture Continuum. It consists of four classes of architectures from the most generic, or foundational, to those specific to an organization.   A relationship exists between the architecture classes. As architectures become more specific in detail, the more the enterprise needs and business requirements are addressed.

The evolutionary transformation is not a formal process and any different type of architecture can be developed at any given point of the continuum. The progression of architecture can be represented

117

on several levels:
- Logical to physical
- IT-focused to business-focused
- General to specific
- Taxonomy to architecture specification

Foundation Architectures are the most generic within the Architecture Continuum and represent an architecture of building blocks and standards that support all Common Systems Architectures and the overall enterprise-operating environment.

Common Systems Architectures select and integrate specific services form the Foundation Architectures to create architecture to build common solutions across several relevant domains. Some common architecture includes security architecture, management architecture, network architecture and the like. A common architecture will address a particular problem domain but not the overall system functionality.

Industry Architectures will integrate common systems components with industry-specific components to create industry solutions for targeted problems for a specific industry customer. Industry architectures reflect the requirements and standards specific to a vertical industry and contain industry-specific data, application, and process models.

Organization-Specific Architectures describe and direct the final deployment of solution components for a specific enterprise or network of connected enterprises. Organization-Specific Architectures build on and adopt the concepts and requirements found in the previous architectures as they apply to enterprise architecture for a specific organization.

9.1.4   Solutions Continuum

The different levels of the Solution Continuum have a direct correspondence with the levels of the Architecture Continuum. In its own right, the Solution Continuum represent the detailed specifications and constructions of architectures found in the Architecture Continuum. The Solution Continuum references the architectures with either solutions building blocks, purchased or custom built. In essence, the Solution Continuum becomes a solutions inventory providing value to managing and implementing improvements to the enterprise. As a rule, the more generic the solution, the greater an enterprise need is addressed; the more specific the solution, the greater chance of providing solutions value.

Foundation Solutions are very generic concepts, tools, products, services, and solutions components, which fundamentally provide capabilities. Services are mostly professional services or support services. Solutions include programming languages, operating systems, foundational data structures, generic approaches, and foundational structures.

Common Systems Solutions are an implementation of a Common Systems Architecture. They consist of a set of products and services, which may be certified or branded. Each solution represents a collection of common requirements and capabilities, providing organizations with operating environments addressing operational or informational needs.

Computer systems vendors typically offer technology-centric Common Systems Solutions. Mosts Cloud Computing services or business process outsourcing are examples of common systems solutions.

Industry Solutions implement Industry Architectures, providing re-usable packages of common components and services specifically designed for an industry. The components are provided by Common systems Solutions and Foundation Solutions and augmented with industry-specific components.

Organization-Specific Solutions provide required business functions and have the greatest amount of unique content needed to meet the needs of several people and processes of specific organizations. The key factors defines within an Organization-Specific Solution are Service Level Agreements, key operating parameters, and quality metrics

9.1.5   Working with TOGAF

The TOGAF ADM is a process description for developing architectures specific to an enterprise and solutions, which conform to the developed architecture. The architecture and solution assets used in development are generally defined or described in the Enterprise Continuum.

TOGAF provides two reference models, which are found in the Enterprise Continuum and available for use during architecture development:
- The TOGAF Foundation Architecture consists of a Technical Reference Model (TRM) of generic services and functions, which demonstrate a firm foundation for building specific architectures and architectural components.
- The Integrated Information Infrastructure Reference Model (III-RM) is based on the TOGAF Foundation Architecture and is designed to realize architectures that enable and support the vision of Boundaryless Information Flow.

9.2   Architecture Partitioning

Partitioning of architecture is an effort to establish or show boundaries between individual architectures or groupings of related architectures for a variety of reasons, such as:
- The complexity involved with addressing all existing problems within a single architecture.
- The conflict that exists between different architecture.

- The ability for specific architects to own and develop specific segments of the overall architecture.
- Enables modular re-use of architecture segments for more effective implementation and improvement of the architecture.

9.2.1 Defining Characteristics

For successful architecture partitioning, the characteristics of both solutions and architectures must be defined. Any number of approaches can be used to provide a definition.

The more common set of characteristics for a solution include:
- Subject Matter – describes the content, structure, and function of the solution
- Time – the expected period of time for a solution's existence
- Maturity/Volatility – the extent of change likely over time for the subject matter and environment

The more common set of characteristics for architecture include:
- Subject Matter – describe specific solutions and consequently inherit objective characteristics represented by the solution.
- Viewpoint – a partial representation of the solution based on stakeholder needs built by architectural domains and specific artifacts.
- Level of Detail – represents the uses of architecture.
- Level of Abstraction – represents how abstracted a specific architecture is from the solution it represents.
- Accuracy – how accurate an architecture is as a description of the solution?

Once the characteristics have been defined to the solutions and architectures, the Enterprise Continuum can be partitioned and organized into a set of related solutions and architecture.

9.2.2 Partitioning the Architecture Landscape

Architectures are used to provide summary views of the state of the enterprise, or Architecture Landscape. The characteristics used to partition the Architecture Landscape include:
- Subject Matter – the primary organizing characteristic for describing the Architecture Landscape.
- Level of Detail -provides a manageable architecture size and complexity.
- Time Period – the expected life based on subject matter and level of detail.
- Viewpoint – represents the requirements to architectures from the stakeholders.
- Accuracy – increases that each architecture view moves through a development cycle.

9.2.3 Partitioning Reference Models

Reference models are architectures that describe particular approaches to solutions, best practices, and patterns that can be shared and developed. The following characteristics are used to partition reference models:
- Level of Abstraction – the greater the abstraction found in a reference model, the more applicable the model is to the entire enterprise; less abstraction, the more specific the areas of the enterprise are addressed.
- Subject Matter – allows ease-of-reference for the subject matter.
- Viewpoint – A specific subject may have several reference models addressing it from different complementary viewpoints.

9.2.4 Partitioning Architectural Standards

Standards are typically defined and mandated by organizations to encourage adoption. Architectural standards are typically partitioned using the following characteristics:

- Viewpoint – 'horizontal' viewpoints starting with the architecture domains.
- Subject Matter – allows grouping of related standards.
- Maturity/Volatility – related to the a standard's lifecycle stage in the enterprise.

9.2.5 Working the ADM

The Preliminary phase of the ADM supports identifying architecture partitions and establishes governance relationships between all related partitions.

Phases A through F allows the architecture to be defines within a specific partition.

Phases G and H allows an architecture implementation to be governed.

9.3 Architecture Repository

The Architecture Repository is a holding area for different types of architectural assets existing within different levels of abstraction. There are six classes of architectural information found in the Architecture Repository:

- Architecture Metamodel
- Architecture Capability
- Architecture Landscape
- Standards Information Base
- Reference Library
- Governance Log

Copyright The Art of Service | Brisbane, Australia | Email:service@theartofservice.com
Web: http://theartofservice.com | eLearning: http://theartofservice.org | Phone: +61 (0)7 3252 2055

9.3.1 Architecture Landscape

The Architecture Landscape is a set of architectural views of the state of the enterprise at specific points in time. The Architecture Landscape has three levels of granularity:
- Strategic Architectures – representing long-term summary views of the entire enterprise.
- Segment Architectures – representing detailed operating models for areas in the enterprise.
- Capability Architectures – representing details on operating options for an enterprise to support a particular unit of capability.

9.3.2 Standards Information Base

The Standards Information Base (SIB) contains a set of specifications, which require conformity from the architectures. The types of standards found include:
- Legal and Regulatory Obligations – mandated by law
- Industry Standards – established by industry bodies
- Organizational Standards – established by the organization

Standards have their own lifecycle and pass through a series of stages, defined as:
- Trial Standard
- Active Standard
- Depreciated Standard
- Obsolete Standard

9.3.3 Reference Library

A Reference Library contains the best practice or template materials used to construct enterprise architecture. A variety of sources may provide reference materials, including:
- Governing bodies for standards
- Product and service vendors
- Industry communities or forums

- Corporately defined templates
- Project implementation best practices

9.3.4   Governance Log

The Governance Log is a repository of shared information related to the ongoing governance of projects, and includes:
- Decision Logs
- Compliance Assessments
- Capability Assessments
- Calendar
- Project Portfolio
- Performance Measurements

10 TOGAF Reference Models

10.1 Technical Reference Model

The Technical Reference Model (TRM) is part of the TOGAF Foundation Architecture, which describes generic platform services. It can be used to develop any system architecture.

Any TRM has two components:
- A taxonomy, which defines the terminology used and provides a consistent description of components and conceptual structure of an information system.
- An associated graphic providing a visual representation of the taxonomy.

10.1.1 TRM Structure

The TRM has two common architectural objectives: Application Portability and Interoperability

The major entities of the TRM are:
- Application Software
- Application Platforms
- Communication Infrastructure

The entities are connected using the Application Platform Interface and the Communication Infrastructure Interface.

Application software is categorized under:
- Business Applications - used to implement business processes for a specific enterprise or vertical industry
- Infrastructure Applications – provides general purpose business functionality

The Application Platform is a single, generic, entity of concept where a set of Application Software sits with the intentional objective of meeting an enterprise's business requirements.

The Application Platform Interface (API) is the connecting component between Application Software and the Application Platform. IT focuses on providing application portability, which requires the conformity of both applications and the platform to the interface. High-level services for the Application Platform are defined as:

- Data Interchange Services
- Data Management Services
- Graphics and Imaging Services
- International Operation Services
- Location and Directory Services
- Network Services
- Operating System Services
- Software Engineering Services
- Transaction Processing Services
- User Interface Services
- Security Services
- System and Network Management Services

Services are provided in a object-oriented manner using an Object Request Broker (ORB) and Common Object services

The Application Platform seeks to fulfill several qualities beneficial to the enterprise, including:

- Availability
- Assurance
- Usability
- Adaptability

The Communications Infrastructure provides the basic services required to interconnect systems and allow the transfer or data. The infrastructure itself is a combination of hardware and software that provide the networking and physical links used by systems.

The Communications Infrastructure Interface connected the Communication Infrastructure with the Application Platform to provide interoperability within the enterprise and with the global community.

The Integrated Information Infrastructure Reference Model (III-RM) is a component and extension of the TOGAF Technical Reference Model which addresses and the ability of an enterprise to enable Boundaryless Information Flow. Like other components of the TOGAF, the IIS-RM is comprised of taxonomy and an associated graphic representing the taxonomy.

10.2.1 Boundaryless Information Flow

The concept of Boundaryless Information Flow has its roots in the modern enterprise's growing need for speed, flexibility, and responsiveness in the organization's ability to work together. The solution is the creation of an infrastructure that integrates the information requirements of the organization and provides integrated access to that information by all members of the organization.

10.2.2 III-RM Structure

The core components of a III-RM at a high-level are:
- Business Applications (BA)
- Infrastructure Applications (IA)
- Application Platform
- Interfaces
- Qualities

The applications are further broken down into:
- Brokering Applications – a business application designed to manage requests fro clients to Information Provider Applications
- Information Provider Applications – a business application, which provides responses to client requests and basic access to data.
- Information Consumer Applications – a business application designed to deliver content to users and request access to information on a specific system.

- Development Tools – an infrastructure application, which provides the necessary modeling, design, and construction capabilities to develop and deploy applications.
- Management Utilities – an infrastructure application providing the necessary utilities to understand operate, tune, and manage the run-time system to meet business demand.

10.2.3 Infrastructure Applications

Infrastructure Applications are comprised on development tools and management utilities by the reference model.

The development tools recognized are represented as:
- Business Modeling Tools – covering tools for modeling business rules and process rules.
- Design Modeling Tools – covering tools for designing, defining, and documenting IT elements of the business based on the business and business models.
- Implementation and Construction Tools – enables the development of re-usable processes, applications, and application services.
- Data Modeling Tools – covering tools for establishing data classifications and relationships.
- Deployment Tools – used for implementing software from the development environment into the operational environment.
- Libraries – supports the re-use of software libraries.

Management utilities recognized are represented as:
- Operations, Administration, and Management (OA&M) Utilities – covers traditional systems management and administrative utilities managing business rules and information objects.
- Quality of Service Manager Utilities – covers health monitoring and management utilities.
- Copy Management Utilities – covering utilities for managing data movement in the enterprise.

Copyright The Art of Service | Brisbane, Australia | Email:service@theartofservice.com
Web: http://theartofservice.com | eLearning: http://theartofservice.org | Phone: +61 (0)7 3252 2055

- Storage Management Utilities – providing least-cost data storage management.

10.2.4 Application Platform Services

Below is a detailed listing of the varied categories of services within the Application Platform component

Software Engineering Services
- Languages
- Libraries
- Registries

Security Services
- Authentication
- Authorization
- Access Control
- Single sign-on
- Digital signature
- Firewall
- Encryption
- Intrusion detection
- Identity management
- Key management

Location and Directory Services
- Directory
- Registration
- Publish/Subscribe
- Discovery
- Naming
- Referencing/dereferencing

Human Interaction Services
- Presentation
- Transformation
- Browser
- Meta Indices
- Portal and personalization

Data Interchange Services
- Information format
- eForm
- Instant Messaging
- Application messaging
- Application-to-application communications
- Enterprise Application integration

Data Management Services
- Information and data access
- Transformation mapping
- Query distribution
- Aggregation
- Search
- File

11 Architecture Capability Framework

The Architecture Capability Framework is a set of reference materials providing guidance on establishing an architecture function within an enterprise. To realize architecture capability, a number of elements must be addressed like organization structures, processes, roles, responsibilities, and skills.

Within the Architecture Capability Framework, specific architectural aspects are supported to ensure that enterprise meets the designed capabilities of the architecture, including:
- Architecture Board
- Architecture Compliance
- Architecture Contracts
- Architecture Governance
- Architecture Maturity Models
- Architecture Skills Framework

11.1 Architecture Board

The Architecture Board is an cross-organization entity overseeing the implementation of the architecture strategy. They should serve as a representation of the entire key stakeholder in the architecture.

They can have a global, regional, or business line scope. Multiple boards may exist within an organization.

11.1.1 Responsibilities

The Architecture Board is typically responsible for:
- Consistency between sub-architectures
- Identifying re-usable components
- Flexibility of enterprise architecture
- Enforcement of Architecture Compliance
- Improving the maturity level of the architecture discipline throughout the organization
- Ensuring the architecture-based development discipline is adopted

- Providing the basis for making decisions around changes to the architecture
- Supporting escalation capabilities for out-of-bound decisions

From an operational perspective, the Architecture Board is responsible for:
- Monitoring and control aspects of the Architecture Contract
- Meeting on a regular basis
- Ensuring effective management and implementation of architectures
- Resolving ambiguities, issues and conflicts
- Providing advice, guidance, and information
- Ensuring architectural compliance and granting dispensations
- Considering policy changes
- Validating reported service level, cost savings, and other concerns

From a governance perspective, the Architecture Board is responsible for:
- Producing usable governance materials and activities
- Providing a mechanism for formal acceptance and approval of architecture
- Providing a control mechanism for effective implementation of the architecture
- Establishing and maintaining the link between strategy, objectives, and implementation of the architecture

11.1.2 Creating an Architecture Board

Architecture Boards are established when:
- New CIO established
- Merger or acquisition
- Consideration of a move to new technology
- Poor alignment between IT and business
- Maintaining competitive advantage
- Creation of an enterprise architecture program

- Significant business change
- Requirement for complex, cross-functional solutions

The recommended size of the Architecture Board is no more than ten, with four or five permanent members being the ideal size. Membership should be rotated to prevent long-term conflicts for some participants. The organization form should be reflected in the Architecture Board structure.

11.1.3 Operation of an Architecture Board

Architecture Board meetings are conducted regularly with clearly defined agendas. Topics of consideration should include:
- Change requests
- Dispensations
- Compliance Assessments
- Resolving Disputes
- Architecture Strategy and Direction documentation
- Assigning Actions
- Contract Documentation Management

11.2 Architecture Compliance

An essential aspect of architecture governance is the compliance of individual projects to the enterprise architecture. Compliance is derived by a solution's ability to:
- Support the stated strategy and future directions
- Adhere to stated standards
- Provide the stated functionality
- Adhere to stated principle

11.2.1 Levels of Architecture Compliance

There are six levels of Architecture Compliance:
- Irrelevant – the implementation and architecture specification has no common features
- Consistent – some common features are common to both the implementation and architecture specification but they are not implemented in accordance to the specification
- Compliant – some features in the architecture specification are not implemented, but all implemented features are in accordance to the specification
- Conformed – All features in the architecture specification are implemented in accordance with the specification, but additional features are implemented not in accordance with it
- Fully Conformed – Only features in the architecture specification are implemented with no additional features outside the specification and all features are implemented in accordance with the specification
- Non-conformed – Any situation will a feature of the architecture specification is implemented but not in accordance to the specification

11.2.2 Architecture Compliance Reviews

Conformity is supported by the Architecture function's ability to prepare a series of Project Impact Assessments and the IT Governance function's ability to define a formal review process.

Project Impact Assessments provides an opportunity to describe how the enterprise architecture affects the projects currently in place in the organization.

Assessments should be conducted at:
- Project initiation
- Initial design
- Architecture development
- Architecture implementation

- Major design changes
- Ad Hoc

11.2.3 Roles of Architecture Compliance Process

The roles involved in the Architecture Compliance process include:
- Architecture Board – ensures consistent IT architecture and support overall business needs
- Project Leader – responsible for the project
- Architecture Review Coordinator – administers the whole architecture development and review process
- Lead Enterprise Architect – ensures the architecture is technically coherent
- Architect – assists the Lead Enterprise Architect
- Customer – ensures business requirements are clearly expressed and understood
- Business Domain Expert – ensure the processes to satisfy business requirements are justified and understood
- Project Principals – ensures the architects have sufficient detailed knowledge of customer processes

11.2.4 Architecture Compliance Review Process

Architecture Compliance Reviews are used to verify the compliance of a specific project against the established architecture criteria, spirit, and business objectives. The steps of the Architecture Compliance Review are:
- Request an architecture review
- Identify responsible parties and project principles
- Identify Lead Architect
- Determine the scope of the review
- Tailor checklists
- Schedule the Architecture Compliance Review meeting
- Interview project principals
- Analyze completed checklists
- Prepare report on the review
- present findings in the report
- Obtain acceptance of findings

136

- Send the assessment report to the Architecture Review Coordinator

Several checklists might be used to guide any effort to determine conformance, including:
- Hardware and Operating System Checklists
- Software Services and Middleware Checklists
- Applications Checklists
- Information Management Checklists
- Security Checklists
- System Management Checklists
- System Engineering/Overall Architecture Checklists
- System Engineering/Methods and Tools Checklists

11.3 Architecture Contracts

Architecture contracts are agreements between development providers and sponsor. The agreements describe the deliverables, quality, and the fitness-for-purpose requirements for the desired development effort.

11.3.1 Role of Architecture Contracts

When managing contracts properly, it ensures:
- Integrity, decision-making, and audit of activities of architecture systems are continuously monitored
- Principles, standards, and requirements of existing or developing architectures are adhered to
- risks related to all aspects of developing and implementing architectures are identified
- Accountability, responsibility, and discipline related to development and usage of artifacts are clearly documented in processes and practices
- A formal understanding of the governance organization

137

11.3.2 Contents of Architecture Contracts

Managing contracts is a function of architecture governance as it ensures that responsibility for development is adequately delegated and accepted throughout the organization. Architecture Contracts are often used to drive architecture change. Different architecture contracts are required during different phases of the Architecture Development Method and include:

- Statement of Architecture Work
- Contract between Architecture Design and Development Partners
- Contract between Architecting Functions and Business Users

11.4 Architecture Governance

Architecture Governance aligns the framework with current best practices and ensures an appropriate level of visibility, guidance and control to support the stakeholder's requirements and obligations.

11.4.1 Benefits of Architecture Governance

- Increases transparency of accountability
- Provides informed delegation of authority
- Provides controlled risk management
- Allows re-use of processes, concepts , and components
- Creates value through monitoring, measuring, evaluation, and feedback
- Increases visibility of decisions at all levels
- Increases shareholder value
- Integrates with existing solutions through control capabilities

11.4.2 Implementation of Architecture Governance

Architecture Governance is generally accepted as a distinct domain within a hierarchy of governance structures, including:
- Corporate governance
- Technology governance
- IT governance
- Architecture governance

Governance has specific characteristics that amplify their value and necessity in an enterprise:
- Discipline – commitment to adhere to procedures, processes, and authority structures
- Transparency – all activity and decision-making structures available to inspection
- Independence - processes, decision-making, and mechanisms are established to minimize and avoid potential conflicts of interest.
- Accountability – groups are authorized and accountable for their actions
- Responsibility – contracted parties required to act responsibly
- Fairness – activities and solutions do not create an unfair advantage to a particular party

11.4.3 Architecture Governance Framework

Conceptually, the Architecture Governance is a set of processes, a cultural orientation, set of owned responsibilities, and an approach for overseeing the integrity and effectiveness of the architecture.

The processes of Architecture Governance include:
- Policy Management – integrates architecture contracts with existing governance content to allow management and auditing
- Compliance – performs assessments against SLAs, OLAs, standards, and regulatory requirements

- Dispensation – used when compliance is not meet by a subject area to provide the responsible party an opportunity to correct
- Monitoring and Reporting - basis of performance management
- Business Control - used to ensure compliance in business policies
- Environment Management – ensures an effective and efficient repository-based environment

The framework for Architecture Governance provides several levels of support within its organizational structure, including:
- Global governance board
- Local governance board
- Design authorities
- Working parties

11.5 Architecture Maturity Models

The Architecture Capability Framework is based on the Capability Maturity Models (CMM), which provides an effective method for enabling an organization to gain control and improve its IT-related development processes in a gradual manner.

Several models are available for use:
- Capability Maturity Model Integration (CMMI)
- Software Acquisition Capability Maturity Model (SA-CMM)
- Systems Engineering Capability Maturity Model (SE-CMM)
- People Capability Maturity Model (P-CMM)
- IDEAL Life Cycle Model for Improvement
- IT Architecture Capabilities Maturity Model (ACMM)

The ACMM is comprised of three sections:
- The IT architecture maturity model
- IT architecture characteristics of processes at different maturity levels
- The ACMM scorecard

11.5.1 Maturity Levels

Six levels of maturity are present for nine architecture characteristics:
- The Levels
  - o 0 None
  - o 1 Initial
  - o 2 Under Development
  - o 3 Defined
  - o 4 Managed
  - o 5 Measured
- The Characteristics
  - o IT architecture process
  - o IT architecture development
  - o Business linkage
  - o Senior management involvement
  - o Operating unit participation
  - o Architecture communication
  - o IT security
  - o Architecture governance
  - o IT investment and acquisition strategy

11.6 Architecture Skills Framework

A skills framework defines:
- Roles within a work area
- Skills required for each role
- Depth of knowledge required for successfully fulfilling each role

From this information, the organization has a method for viewing the competency levels required for the roles within the architecture.

11.6.1 Benefits of the Skills Framework

The benefits for using the TOGAF Architecture Skills Framework include:
- Reduced time, cost, and risk in hiring, training, and managing personnel
- Reduced time and cost to set up an internal architecture practice
- Reduced time and cost to the overall solution development

TOGAF Roles

The makeup of a typical architecture team includes the following roles:
- Architecture Board Members
- Architecture Sponsor
- Architecture Manager
- Enterprise Architects
- Business Architects
- Data Architects
- Application Architects
- Technology Architects
- Program and/or Project Managers
- IT Designers

11.6.2 Skill Categories

Skills are generally categorized as:
- Generic Skills
- Business Skills and Methods
- Enterprise Architecture Skills
- Program and Project Management Skills
- IT General Knowledge Skills
- Technical IT Skills
- Legal Environment

11.6.3 Proficiency Levels

There are four levels of knowledge or proficiency in any area recognized by the TOGAF Architecture Skills Framework:
- Level 1: Background – Not a required skill
- Level 2: Awareness – Understands background, issues, and implications sufficiently
- Level 3: Knowledge – Detailed knowledge of subject area
- Level 4: Extensive practical experience and applied knowledge

12 Glossary

Abstraction – a technique of describing detailed and complex content in a generalized fashion.

Activity – A task or collection of tasks supporting organizational functions.

Actor – a person, organization, or system, which initiates or interacts with activities.

Application – an operational IT system supporting business functions and services.

Application Architecture – a description of logical groupings of capabilities used to manage the data objects required support the business.

Application Platform – a collection of technology components of hardware and software used to support applications.

Application Platform Interface (API) – an interface or set of functions, between the application software and application platform.

Architectural Style – distinctive features showing how architectures perform.

Architecture – 1) a formal description of a system or detailed plan of a system at the component level to aid implementation. 2) The structure of components, relationships, principles, and guidelines, which govern design and growth over time.

Architecture Building Block (ABB) – a form of the architecture model.

Architecture Continuum – a part of the Enterprise Continuum comprising of a repository of architectural elements.

Architecture Development Method (ADM) – a formal approach to develop and use an enterprise architecture

Architecture Domain – and specific area of the architecture where development focus can reside. Four domains exist within TOGAF: business, data, application, and technology.

Architecture Framework – a structure or set of structures used to develop different architectures.

Architecture Governance – the practice and orientation for managing and controlling architectures at an enterprise level.

Architecture Principles – a statement of intent used to identify requirements for the architecture.

Architecture View – a defined perspective of the architecture.

Architecture Vision – 1) a high-level view of the Target Architecture. 2) A phase in the ADM defining the Architecture Vision. 3) A specific deliverable of the Architecture Vision phase.

Artifact – an architectural work product describing the architecture from a specific viewpoint.

Baseline – A formally reviewed and agreed upon specification, which serves as the basis fro development or change.

Boundaryless Information Flow – 1) The Open Group trademark. 2) a representation of the desired state of the information infrastructure to support the business needs of the organization through combining multiple sources of information and delivering secured information across the enterprise.

Building Block – represents a component of business, IT, or architectural capability, which is combined with other building blocks to deliver architectures and solutions.

Business Architecture – a combination and interactions of business strategy, governance, organization, and key business processes.

Business Domain – a grouping of coherent business functions and activities.

Business Function – a identifiable component, which delivers business capabilities, aligned to the needs of an organization.

Business Governance – ensures the business processes and policies adhere to relevant regulatory standard sand delivers expected business outcomes.

Business Service – an explicitly defined interface supporting business capabilities and governed by the organization.

Capability – the ability possessed by an organization, person, or system, which are defined in general terms.

Capability Architecture – a detailed description of the architectural approach to realize a particular solution or aspect of a solution.

Capability Increment – the output of a business change initiative delivering an increase in performance.

Communications and Stakeholder Management – the process and discipline of managing the needs of the stakeholders of the enterprise architecture and the execution of communication required.

Concerns – the key interests of the stakeholder in a system, which determine the acceptance of the system in the enterprise.

Constraints – any external factor, which prevents an organization from utilizing a specific approach to meet its goals.

Data Architecture – the structure of the logical and physical data assets and data management resources within an organization.

Deliverable – an architectural work product, which is specified contractually and represents the output of projects.

Enterprise – the description of an organization at the highest level covering all missions and functions.

Enterprise Continuum - a mechanism used to classify architecture and solution artifacts.

Environment Management – the processes and discipline to manage the environment required to support the operations of the enterprise architecture practice.

Financial Management – the processes and discipline to manage the financial aspects of the enterprise architecture practice.

Foundation Architecture – an set of generic services and functions used to build specific architectures and architectural components.

Framework – a structure for content or process used to provide consistency and completeness to a solution.

Gap – the statement of the difference between a baseline and target state of a focused area.

Governance – the discipline of monitoring, managing, and steering business activities to achieve desired business outcomes.

Information – a representation of facts, data, or opinions gathered for sharing.

Information Technology (IT) – 1) the lifecycle management of information and related technology within an organization. 2) A terms used to represent the subject areas related to a computer environment. 3) A term assigned to a department tasked with providing services and support to a computer environment.

Interoperability – the ability to share information and services between departments, systems, or functions.

Knowledge – the awareness and understanding of information gained int eh form of experience or learning.

Logical – a definition of the architecture, which is independent of any implementation and typically, involves the grouping related physical

146

entities based on their purpose and structure.

Metadata – data about data, which describes the characteristics of an entity.

Metamodel – a structured method describing an architecture.

Method – a defined, repeatable approach to address a specific problem type.

Methodology – a defined, repeatable series of steps to address a particular problem type centering on a specific process.

Model – a representation of a subject of interest on a smaller scales, more simplified, and/or abstractual.

Modeling – a technique though the construction of models enabling a subject to be represented.

Objective – a time-bound milestone demonstrating progress towards a goal.

Organization – a self-contained unit of resources with defined responsibility, goals, objectives, and measures.

Patterns – a technique for combining building blocks into a useful context.

Performance Management – the monitoring, control, and reporting of the performance of a enterprise architecture.

Physical – a description of a real-world entity.

Platform – a combination of technology products and components used to host application software.

Platform Services – the technical capability required to provide the requirement infrastructure for supporting applications.

Principles – general rules and guidelines intended to inform and support the organization's fulfillment of its mission.

Reference Model – an abstract framework for understanding significant relationships between entities of an environment and to develop consistent standards or specification supporting that environment.

Repository – a system for manging the data of an enterprise.

Requirement – a statement of business need that must be met by a particular architecture or work package.

Resource Management – the acquisition, development, and management of human resources within the enterprise architecture.

Roadmap – an abstracted plan for business or technology change.

147

Role – 1) the usual or expected function of an actor. 2) The part an individual plays in an organization and the contribution made through skills, knowledge, experience, and abilities.

Segment Management – the process and discipline of the execution and performance of enterprise architecture services.

Service Orientation – a perspective formed by service terms and service-based development and the outcomes of services.

Service Oriented Architecture (SOA) – an architectural style based on the design of services, representing those services through the context provided by business descriptions, placing unique requirements on the infrastructure, and providing environment-specific implementations. SOA requires strong governance of service definition, representation, and implementation.

Skill – the ability to perform a job-specific activity.

Solution Architecture – a description of discrete and focused business operations and activities and the IT supporting that operation.

Solution Building Blocks – a physical solution for an Architecture Building Block.

Solutions Continuum – a part of the Enterprise Continuum representing a repository of re-usable solutions for future implementations.

Stakeholder – an individual, team, or organization with particular interests or concerns for the outcome of an architecture.

Standards Information Base (SIB) – a database of standards used to define the particular services and components of an organization-specific architecture.

Strategic Architecture – a formal description of the enterprise, providing an organizing framework for operational and change activity and direction setting.

Target Architecture – the description of a future state of the architecture being developed for an organization.

Taxonomy or Architecture Views – the organized collection of all views pertinent to an architecture.

Technical Reference Model (TRM) – a structure for describing the components of an information system in a consistent manner.

Technology Architecture – the logical software and hardware capabilities required to support deployment of business, data, and

148

application services.

Transition Architecture – a formal description of the enterprise architecture showing periods of transition and development for sections of the enterprise.

View – a representation of a related set of concerns.

Viewpoint – a definition of the perspective using a specific view.

Work Package – a set of actions used to achieve one or more business objectives.

Copyright The Art of Service | Brisbane, Australia | Email:service@theartofservice.com
Web: http://theartofservice.com | eLearning: http://theartofservice.org | Phone: +61 (0)7 3252 2055

13 Practice Exam

The following multiple-choice questions are a refresher from the Foundation level as a prelude.

Question 1

You are an Architect Lead with a major retailing organization. The company has recently made an effort to expand their product lines across the board and in so doing have made several agreements with new vendors. In an effort to save costs by streamlining processes, they have submitted a Request for Architecture Work. In the request, operations management has requested a IT solution, which connects the various vendors, old and new, to the company's procurement and processing system. Such a connection exists for one major vendor with the greatest level of satisfaction from all stakeholders and they were hoping to duplicate. As the Lead Architect, what is the most reasonable course of action to take?

A) Following through with the ADM, the initial steps will consist of aligning the request with the current principles and goals of the enterprise architecture to create a Statement of Work. Since, the solution type request is already in place fro one vendor, the information on that connection should be retrieved from the Enterprise Continuum. Working with the other vendors, common features in the different architectures to support a solution must be identified. Using a matrix, these common features should be analyzed for compliance to the existing solution and the ease of implementation. The Statement of Work and Architecture Design Document are updated and presented to the project stakeholders within the company and vendors to obtain agreement to move forward.

B) Using the ADM, the Architect Lead ensures that the submitted request is scoped accurately and the appropriate stakeholders in the company and vendors are identified. The Statement of Architecture Work should be started and updated as more information is obtained. The Enterprise Continuum is reviewed to identify the architecture and solution supporting the existing company/vendor connection. An initial gap analysis should be performed with the other vendors to understand the requirements to replicate the connection to each new vendor, as well as a risk analysis to identify the associated risks involved with each connection. The Statement of Architecture Work should be updated, especially with an expected schedule for adding connections to the solution starting with the most number of common elements with specific vendors. This schedule is communicated to the stakeholders to set expectations.

C) The Architect Lead represents the change request to the Architecture Board with supporting information from the Enterprise Continuum about the existing successful pattern and associated business goals, principles, and strategic drivers with the intention of obtaining consensus to move forward. Using the ADM, stakeholders for the project and additional concerns are identified. Gap analysis is performed with each vendor to identify the number of common architecture and solution elements with the accepted pattern and the associated risk s involved with replicated the pattern with the vendor. The Statement of Architecture Work is developed with the final architecture design and expected implementation requirements for each vendor. Each implementation with a vendor should be represented within an overall Transition and Migration Plan, which is overseen by the Architecture Board.

D) The Architect Lead represents the change request to the Architecture Board with supporting information from the Solution Continuum about the existing successful solution and associated business goals, principles, and strategic drivers relevant to promote into the environment. Using the ADM, a solution is developed which incorporates the SBBs of the existing connection and supports the future connections with the additional vendors. A gap analysis is initiated with each vendor to identify the implementation requirements to apply the solution to each connection. A priority list provides the basis to establish a migration plan for adding connections to the overall architecture.

Question 2

A leading firm within the health care industry is looking at ways to expand their business into new markets. Some of these markets have different regulatory expectations specifically in the area of confidential patient information and availability of records. In addition to these new regulations, existing regulations that the firm already operates under are changing to provide more effective standards for interoperability between health care entities.

The CIO recognizes that the additional requirements may have a significant impact on the existing IT solution and is aware that the current solution is running at capacity. Any change may require sufficient capital expenditure to ensure that the requirements can be met. The Board of Directors have agreed with his assessment and granted him some space to get the work complete if the implemented solution also ensures that the IT capabilities remain flexible and adaptive to the changing environment of the health care industry in the next five to ten years.

He brings these new requirements and expectations to the Architecture Board and the effort is assigned to a Lead Architect. What is the best course of action to be taken given the general requirements stated?

A) The Lead Architect should engage the stakeholders of the current IT implementation to review the new requirements and identify any additional concerns specific to the performance, capacity, and security of the future architecture. Next, the security architect should be engaged to assist in translating the new requirements and concerns into realistic architecture requirements. The new architecture should be compared to the baseline architecture to identify gaps and determine the necessary steps to implement and migrate the target architecture. A risk analysis and threat analysis should be performed in the environment against the security measures required to comply with the new regulations. The output of these efforts should be incorporated into the Architecture Design. The final deliverables, including an Implementation and Migration Plan, should be reviewed and accepted by the stakeholders and the Architecture Board.

B) The Lead Architect should engage the stakeholders of the current IT implementation as soon as possible, to review the new requirements and identify any concerns with those requirements as well as concerns with the current IT implementation in terms of capacity and performance. Using the original requirements and additional concerns as acceptance criteria for a target architecture, the baseline architecture should be assessed and a gap analysis performed to identify the effort required to make a architectural change. A viable Target Architecture, Implementation and Migration Plan, and supporting documentation should be created and reviewed by the stakeholders and Architecture Board for acceptance.

C) The Lead Architect should engage the stakeholders of the current IT implementation as soon as possible to review the new requirements and identify any concerns with those requirements as well as any performance and capacity concerns with the current IT implementation. The original requirements and stakeholder concerns are translated into architectural requirements, which are compared with the baseline architecture to identify which are currently being fulfilled by the existing infrastructure. A target architecture is developed with a proposed migration plan. These deliverables are presented to the stakeholders for acceptance and then assigned a project manager to implement.

D) The Lead Architect should engage the stakeholders of the current IT implementation to review the new requirements and identify any additional concerns specific to the performance and capacity of the future iteration of the IT implementation. The original requirements and concerns are translated into architecture requirements. The security architect is engaged to review the architecture requirements and supply any compliance elements needed because of the new direction. The final architecture requirements with security focus is compared to the baseline to identify the gaps required to meet the target architecture. These gaps are translated into implementation tasks and prioritize under a Migration Plan. The final deliverables representing the architecture and plan for implementation are presented to the stakeholder for acceptance.

Question 3

You have been hired as an Enterprise Architect for a established company that has done a major transformation of their services support based on the principles of Service Oriented Architecture. The reasons for their services approach stemmed from a need to improve customer service and position the company strongly in the competitive market. Though some positive results have occurred in these areas, the operating costs of the company has increased and several issues have been identified concerning difficulties in communications between new business services. A recent business study has identified a severe disconnect between business operations and the IT infrastructure

As the new Enterprise Architect, you have been tasked with identifying improvements to the current situation and presenting a viable plan to align IT solutions with business goals. What is the best approach using TOGAF to support the SOA initiative?

A) Identify the stakeholders in each of the service and discuss the situation to identify concerns and possible improvements that they feel need to be done within their service line. Perform an assessment of the services to identify those services directly and indirectly supporting critical business functions. Design and build IT solutions that will promote communication within and between the service lines supporting these business functions.

B) Identify the technological functions and their criticality to business services currently in existence in the environment. With the assistance of the stakeholders, create an architecture model that represents the technological capability to meet the business' core mission. Assess the maturity of each service to meet the conditions set by the model and create a plan for improvement to raise the maturity within each service.

C) Identify the business functions supported by the technology and their criticality to the overall business strategy and goals. Create an hierarchical model of business services to represent the business strategy and the relationships between the various services in the company. Ensure that the various stakeholders within each service line has input and are in agreement with the model. Identify the information systems and technological requirements needed to support the model consistently and assess each service line to identify their capability against those requirements. Defined a general set of shared performance measures to identify how the IT infrastructure is supporting business functions and create a plan for improvement to raise the capabilities of the architecture, specifically starting with the most critical business functions. Store all assessment, measurements, and planning information in a central database, which is assessable by all key stakeholders.

D) Identify the business functions supported by the technology and their criticality as they relate to the overall business strategy and goals. Work with the stakeholders in each business function to identify and define the principles, constraints, standards, and patterns and store this information with a central database shared between the different service lines. Create an hierarchical model of the business services, which represents the relationships between the various services relative to strategy and goals of the company. Define a set of performance measures for each service line to identify their capability to effectively support the business and work with other services lines in the organization. Perform maturity assessments on each service line to establish their baseline effectiveness. With input from the stakeholders, create a series of improvement proposals for information systems and technology to raise the maturity of the service lines, with the primary intent to adopt re-usable architecture and solution components across the business to reduce cost and increase interoperability.

Question 4

A rapidly growing company has recently performed an internal evaluation of its operations in respect to technology and its alignment to business goals. The evaluation had some encouraging discoveries about the commitment to a positive business image and to increasing the marketability of the business to the customer base.
Unfortunately, the evaluation also showed that very little control was in place for technology use or guidance in decision-making, making the costs of operation extremely high and the solutions in place being implemented in isolations within specific business lines.

The CIO has asked you to provide a proposal for addressing the issues identified in the evaluation from the perspective of TOGAF. What are your recommendations?

A)   Review the business strategy, goals, and objectives of the company and ensure they have been communicated and accepted by key decision makers within the organization. Identify the key drivers for business decisions about technology and information systems, current and future. Assess the current technological solutions in place to identify their capabilities relative to the new driver's o the business and how the solutions fulfill business objectives. Work with stakeholders in each of the business lines to identify areas of improvements, specifically consolidation of redundant or similar systems, inexpensive solutions with better flexibility and adaptive properties, and non-critical legacy systems. Establish a governance body and procedure in the form of an Architecture Board to review all proposed changes to the technological environment in terms of meeting business objectives.

B)   Review the business strategy, goals, and objectives with key stakeholders and the Architecture Board to create a set of governing principles for each of the architecture domains. Using these principles as the basis for evaluation, assess the current technology infrastructure in its capability to meet business objectives. Prioritize the areas that do not comply with these principles based on their critical nature to the business, current operating cost, and difficulty in resolving compliance. Create a plan with the key stakeholders for transitioning the architecture to support these principles and the business objectives behind them. Establish a governance procedure to allow the Architecture Board to review and approve any major change to the technology information to ensure the proposed change adheres to the principles and supports business objectives.

C) Though the commitment of the workforce and management is encouraging, the lack of control in technology decisions must be reigned in. The establishment of an Architecture Board will allow changes to the technological infrastructure to be reviewed and approved is a systematic and structure way to ensure the technology change is truly required and financially viable. Assessments of the current technology solutions should be conducted to identify areas of consolidation or improvements geared to reducing costs and promoting interoperability between business lines.

D) Review the business strategy, goals, and objectives of the company and ensure they have been communicated and accepted by key decision makers within the organization. Identify the key drivers in the business relevant to the decisions made around information systems and technology use across the organization. Assess the current technological solutions in place to identify their capabilities to fulfill business goals and the relevant drivers for using the implemented technologies. Establish a governance procedure for future changes to the technology, which requires all proposals to be reviewed and approved by an Architecture Board based on business strategy and drivers. Identify areas of improvement to reduce costs and increase interoperability in the company.

Question 5

A medium sized company with offices in five U.S. cities has made a recent decision to cut costs in several major areas of the business. The decisions for where to cut costs have been placed primarily on the managers and their respective areas or function they control. Though some savings have been realized, the total reduction in operating costs has not been significant enough. Some transformation of business processes has also occurred at individual offices or common functions, such as human resources, which has led to another reduction of operating costs.

The CIO believes that the area with the greatest potential of cost reduction is within the architecture, specifically identifying and promoting the use of re-usable solutions between office sites. He believes that having similar architectures and solutions will not only reduce cost, but also promote cooperation and business opportunities between different departments. Unfortunately, not everyone agrees especially those managers who are very attached to there current way of doing business.

You have been brought in to assist the CIO in identifying the most appropriate architecture for the company. How would you accomplish this?

A) Using the ADM as a guide for developing the architecture, identify the business goals, principles, and objectives that will be used to define the requirements for the business, information systems, and technical architectures for the company. Based on these requirements and input from key stakeholders, identify the Baseline and Target Architectures for each company site. Perform maturity assessments and gap analysis to identify the effort required to implementation the target architecture and brings similar functions at different locations into a consistent operating mode. Identify the several viewpoints for communicating the Target Architecture to the various stakeholders, including the timelines and resources required to reach the desired state. Ensure that stakeholders are informed and accept the Implementation and Migration Plan.

B) Identify the current architectures and solutions utilized in the environment at each of the location. Perform a cost/benefit analysis to determine the value proposition of each implemented solution, specifically starting with those systems critical to business operations. Prioritize the assessed solutions showing the most critical/least value of the systems first. Use the ADM to design improvements to the architecture using the priority list for guidance and develop a model to show the benefits of the new target architecture. Create an implementation and migration plan with an identified critical path and schedule. With aid from the CIO, present the model and plan to executive management and representatives for each site with the intent to inform and obtain agreement to move forward.

C) Identify the major stakeholders within the company who would be impacted by any architectural effort, specifically identifying those stakeholders whose involvement is critical to the success of the effort. Make an analysis of each stakeholder's commitment to a change in the overall enterprise architecture. Based on this analysis, determine the level of engagement to be taken during the development of the architecture. Using the ADM, obtain the concerns and requirements of the business and each stakeholder. Create Baseline and Target Architectures to identify the desired architecture model and the effort required to reach it. Create specific viewpoints and views that focus on showing the key stakeholder's concerns being clearly addressed by the target architecture. At each major milestone within the ADM, engage the stakeholders appropriately and make a new assessment of their commitment to the effort, adjusting appropriately based on any changes in attitude.

D) Identify the major stakeholders within the company, specifically those with the greatest influence on the decision to move forward and those affected the most by any architectural effort. Work with each of the stakeholders' concerns about the current business and how it is being supported by the enterprise architecture. Develop a model of the baseline architecture and determine how it currently meets the concerns of the various stakeholders and new business requirements. Develop a Target Architecture, which does meet the requirements and concerns presented and identify the appropriate viewpoints for presenting the new architecture and its benefits. With the stakeholders input, identify the most critical areas for moving forward and develop a plan for migrating to the new architecture.

Question 6

You work for a major service company, which is growing quickly and moving into several new markets. Until recently, little focus was placed on creating a viable technology plan or unified solution across the enterprise. In last quarter's planning meeting, it was recognized that for the business objectives to be fulfilled now, and in the future, the IT infrastructure will have to undergo a transformation and applied governance.

Your new responsibility is to project manage an effort to determine the future architecture for the company and provide a proposed Implementation plan. You already have full support of the effort from the key stakeholders and a Target Architecture in each of the four domains that has been accepted by these stakeholders. The only problem is a concern that the implementation of the architecture may not meet expectations within the transitional period without the proper guidance or planning.

What is the best approach to resolve these concerns related to the implementation and migration of the new architecture?

A)   To address the stakeholders concern around the success of the implementation, two major actions must be performed. First, the Implementation Factor Assessment and Deduction Matrix must be completed to identify the existing factors that can affect the implementation and all actions or constraints identified in the matrix incorporated into the Implementation and Migration Plan. The second action is to aid the stakeholder in understanding the expected outcomes at different stages of the implementation, especially on business and technical services. This can be done through the Enterprise Architecture State Evolution Table.

B)   To ensure that the planning of the implementation is successful, all the architecture work packages required must be clearly defined and prioritized. The best course of action is to complete the Consolidated Gaps, Solutions, and Dependencies Matrix to identify what is required to approach the target architecture in the most efficient and effective manner.

C) To address the stakeholders concern around the success of the implementation, two major actions must be performed. First, the Implementation Factor Assessment and Deduction Matrix must be completed to identify the existing factors that can affect the implementation and all actions or constraints identified in the matrix incorporated into the Implementation and Migration Plan. The second action is to have a clear and incremental plan in place to move forward and allow go/no go decisions to be made on smaller aspects of the implementation without affecting the entire effort. This can be done using an Architecture Definition increments Table.

D) The stakeholders have a concern about the success of the implementation, so the best course of action is identify those factors, which can affect the implementation effort. To do this, complete the Implementation Factor Assessment and Deduction Matrix. Incorporate the actions and constraints identified into the Implementation and Migration Plan.

Question 7

You work for a consulting firm, which specializes in building enterprise architectures using a variety of methods including TOGAF. You have been assigned to a new account for a company that is looking to restructure its entire organization. Your involvement is to provide recommendations specific to the IT architecture supporting the business.

In the initial meeting with the company representatives, you receive a fair amount of information related to the business strategy, plans, and objectives of the company, as well as the reasons behind the restructuring. The major issues mentioned include:

1. A number of application and technical solutions current in place are legacy products that are maintained in isolation of the distributed environment. As a result, this is a lack in consistency in the support for these solutions leading to high cost in maintenance and support.
2. A number of unauthorized changes are prevalent in the environment.
3. Communications between departments and from IT to business is confusing and heavy with explanation due to the varying uses in terminology.

The company would like to have immediate results in addressing these issues. You will be working with the Lead Architect and his architecture team to provide recommendations and direction using TOGAF distinctions. The success with these issues will determine if the company will continue their partnership with the firm.

What direction would you give to the architecture team to immediately address the issues?

A) Develop Service Contracts for each of the application and technical solutions to ensure that all support is provided through centralized technical services, which will provide greater consistency in support and decrease operational costs. As part of the Service Contract, a provision to adopt and utilize a change management process is inserted. The Service Contract will provide the foundation for defining common terms within the business as they relate to IT.

B) Working within Preliminary Phase of the ADM, focus on the immediate concerns of governance, communication and adoption of a common language, and identifying the impact of changes to legacy products and their support on the business. This can be accomplished through the development or documentation of the governance framework supporting change management, the architecture framework including the Architecture Repository, and scoping the architectural work.

C) Define a governance and support framework for the architecture, which covers the required change management oversight for the organization. In addition, define the architecture framework to establish a common set of processes, terminologies, and architectural content. Ensure that all stakeholders understand and agree on adopting the frameworks defined

D) Working within the Preliminary Phase of the ADM, identify and establish the architecture principles. Evaluate the legacy products against those principles to identify the context of their implementation in the new architecture and potential improvements required. Establish and promote a governance framework to ensure changes in the environment are managed properly. Tailor the existing architecture framework to identify and potentially resolve any conflicts in language, processes, and architectural content.

Question 8

You have been hired by a startup company with a strong value proposition for their business. Executive management recognizes that the enterprise architecture is a key success factor for the business. You have an Greenfield opportunity to develop and implement the architecture. You have identified the key stakeholders and worked with them to identify the business principles, goals, and requirements relevant to the architecture. You have been given the task to recommend any solution within this context. What are your next steps?

A) Develop an architecture model using common architectural components showing the linkages between IT and critical business functions. In connection to the model, create the various viewpoints and views to understand and manage the architecture, as well as the key performance indicators supporting the business. Identify the risks and benefits for each architecture component. Ensure the model is understood and acceptable to the key stakeholders.

B) A baseline assessment of the current environment must be conducted to identify the current problem areas and opportunities for improvement already present. From this assessment, the weakest areas should be prioritized according to their impact to the critical business practices. Target solutions to strengthen and mature these areas should be identified and applied to the architecture model. These solutions should be reviewed and approved by the key stakeholders before

C) Identify the Architecture and Solution Building Blocks appropriate to addressing the agreed upon business requirements. At first, the ABBs should be as organization specific as possible while the SBBs remain as common systems or industry specific solutions: this is to allows for the greatest level of addressing the enterprise needs of the new business. The core building blocks should be combined and documented to address critical business functions. The key stakeholders should review and accept the recommended architectures and solutions.

Copyright The Art of Service | Brisbane, Australia | Email:service@theartofservice.com
Web: http://theartofservice.com | eLearning: http://theartofservice.org | Phone: +61 (0)7 3252 2055

D) Evaluate the current business capabilities and the business' readiness to undertake architectural change. Develop a series of business scenarios supported by an Architecture Vision. Clearly define the initial risks of transforming the business and creating any relevant mitigation plans. Develop the work products necessary to build an appropriate architecture, ensuring that they match the business performance requirements. The information obtained should be documented in a Statement of Architecture Work and accepted by the stakeholders.

14 Answer Guide

Question 1

Question Rationale		The intent of the question is to recognize and incorporate a successful pattern using the ADM appropriately.
Most Correct	C	This is the best answer for three reasons: 1) it uses the input of the stakeholders and Architecture Board through out the process, especially in the beginning and as oversight for the implementation. 2) It utilizes the architecture and solution patterns within the Enterprise Continuum to fulfill the request. 3) It recognizes the need to implementation in Transitional phases.
Second Best	B	This is a good representation of what must be done. Where it differs from the best answer is its specific intention to perform the work in transitional phase and for the oversight provided by the Architecture Board.
Third Best	A	At the start of the effort in this answer, the stakeholders are not identified or worked with. IT is not until the end that they are engaged.
Distracter	D	Any implementation consists of both an architecture and a solution. This answer focuses heavily on the solution with little to no regard for the architecture.

Question 2

Question Rationale		The question focuses on interacting with changing security requirements
Most Correct	A	This is the best answer because it concentrates on the security aspect of the new regulatory requirements from the very beginning by attempting to identify stakeholder concerns related to security. In addition, the security lead is participating in the formation of the architecture requirements, not reviewing. Finally, the risk and threat analysis effort should be able to identify any additional issues that may exist in the environment specific to the security requirements.
Second Best	D	This answer also engages the security architect, but later in the process than the previous answer and the role is used more as a consultant than an active participant in designing the architecture.
Third Best	B	This answer does not have any mention of the need to focus on security concerns from the new requirements. It does provide the basic and necessary steps for introducing a change to the environment, primarily a gap analysis to aid in transitioning the target architecture.
Distracter	C	This is the worst answer out of the possible choices because to does not consider the security aspect of the problem and provides a more generalized description of the effort. Additionally, the assignment for a project manager is rather late, even if the focus of the project is just the implementation. A project manager should be involved at the very beginning.

Question 3

Question Rationale		The question focuses on supporting Service Oriented Architectures using principles of TOGAF.
Most Correct	D	Using Enterprise Architecture to support SOA initiatives provides four key initiatives, which this answer has: 1) a structured representation of business and technology and their interdependencies. (Hierarchical business model) 2) an Enterprise Continuum and its contents of principles, constraints, frameworks, patterns, and standards. (Central database) 3) a consistent model to address multiple perspectives and problem domains. (Hierarchical business model) 4) A method of governance over deliverables, planning, and analysis (performance measurements, maturity assessment and improvement proposals)
Second Best	C	This is the second best answer primarily because there is no clear indication that the principles of an Enterprise Continuum are being adopted.
Third Best	B	This answer is not close to being as defined as the previous two and focuses mostly on the technology of the company. However, it will provide a good foundation for meeting the expected goals once mapped to business strategy.
Distracter	A	This answer plays out as a series of unattached efforts to attempt to improve the overall standing. Except for the focus on communication, it does little to meet the overall set of problems described in the scenario.

Question 4

Question Rationale		The question focuses on the providing the foundation for proper decision making for technological solutions. For TOGAF, this foundation resides in the development of principles, which in cooperation with the business objectives provides a firm test of a specific solution's capability to support the business appropriately.
Most Correct	B	This is the only answer that specifically creates architecture principals for the company. The principles themselves incorporate the business objectives and the drivers that influence decision-making. They serve as the baseline to determine past decisions as they relate to the current business model and provide guidance for future decisions in technology. The establishment of the Architecture Board allows the principles to be adhered to and where conflicts exist, to make decisions. Improvements are identified through the efforts of the stakeholders, not the single authoritative group or person.
Second Best	A	This answer is very similar to the previous, except that it does not focus on the creation of principles, but rather relies on the external drivers of decisions. Though external drivers do exist, principles are an internal creation providing guidance. Principles should appropriate incorporate external drivers to or provide a substantial level of resistance to those drivers. An Architecture Board is established for governance and stakeholders have a say in improvements to the current environment.
Third Best	D	Though similar in effort to the previous answer, one major disconnect is apparent: there is little or no participation by the stakeholders. Even the creation of the improvement plan seems in isolation from the organization.
Distracter	C	This answer provides a high level of granularity which is not enough to clearly see whether the a resolution can be obtained. The efforts themselves seem to address the issues, but not significantly enough to promote trust or cooperation.

Question 5

Question Rationale		The focus of the question is on stakeholder management. The cultural and political aspects of an organization can deter or advance any architectural effort. The key to success is identifying the potential obstacles that may exist from various, and influential, stakeholders.
Most Correct	C	Stakeholder management contains four major steps, which are demonstrated in this answer. 1) Identify stakeholders. 2) Determine the stakeholder's readiness (commitment) to support the effort. 3) Determine the approach for managing stakeholders. 4) Tailor the deliverables for engagement (Views and viewpoints).
Second Best	D	This answer identifies the stakeholders and tailors the deliverables (viewpoints) to communicate with the stakeholder. However, the answer does not address determining the stakeholder's commitment or determining the proper approach for engaging the stakeholder's.
Third Best	A	Like the previous answer, the stakeholder's are identified and viewpoints are created. The difference from the previous answer is when the stakeholders are engaged, namely after identifying the business goals, principles, and objectives rather than before. Especially in environments where stakeholder issues exist, the earlier they are involved, the greater success experience throughout the effort.
Distracter	B	This answer has very little involvement from the stakeholders.

Question 6

Question Rationale		This question focuses on the Migration Plan and incidental support of that plan. The concerns of the stakeholders can be narrowed down to two major points: what can prevent successful implementation of the architecture and how do we know if successful implementation is threatened.
Most Correct	A	This answer provides two tools to address the points mentioned above. The Implementation Factor Assessment and Deduction Matrix provide a clear presentation of the positive and negative factors that can affect the implementation and migration plan. The Enterprise Architecture State Evolution Table provides a pre-determined view of the progressing enterprise architecture, which can be used to inform the stakeholders what to expect at each stage of the migration.
Second Best	C	Like the previous answer, the Implementation Factor Assessment and Deduction Matrix provide a list of factors, which may affect the implementation. The second tool used is the Architecture Definition Increments Table, which allows deliverables to be assigned to specific transition architecture allowing some control of the implementation plan. This is not the better solution as the second table does not set expectations for the stakeholders, but the provision for more control during implementation provides a good approach.
Third Best	D	This answer only focuses on identifying impact factors on the implementation with the intent to mitigate any problems that could occur.
Distracter	B	Though the Consolidated Gaps, Solutions and Dependencies Matrix can provide a good resource in creating the plan, it does little to address the concerns of the stakeholders.

Question 7

Question Rationale		The focus of this question is the activities of the Preliminary Phase to provide immediate attention to business and technical operations issues.
Most Correct	D	There are several steps in involved in the Preliminary Phase, but the ones listed in the answer have the greatest focus for addressing the issues mentioned. Each of the recommendations has immediate impact and long lasting support for the rest of the ADM. The governance framework provides the change management aspect required by the issues, just as the tailoring of the architecture framework. The definition of principles provides a context for viewing current solutions, including legacy, and assessing their implications on the overall architecture. By focusing in the principles, the architecture team can address in a variety of ways the lack of consistency in support and even validate the need for improvement in legacy solutions from a business context.
Second Best	B	This answer is very similar to the previous answer except that principles are not a focus for addressing the issues. As a result, the issue related to legacy systems is not appropriately handled.
Third Best	C	Like the previous answer, the issue related to legacy systems is not directly addressed. The remaining recommendation are valid but are identified as individual efforts outside the context of the ADM. The result is a disconnect from the larger architectural effort required by the architecture team.
Distracter	A	Service contracts are a viable option for communicating and agreeing to operational terms; however, these the use of these contracts is premature without a clearer understanding of the architecture.

Question 8

Question Rationale		The purpose of this question is to demonstrate possible approaches in a greenfield situation assuming the activities of the preliminary phase are complete.
Most Correct	D	This answer describes activities directly from the Architecture Vision phase. Though it does not provide specific solutions to implement, it provides the foundational structure for communicating and developing the architecture and associated solutions in an iterative fashion.
Second Best	C	This answer attempts to find appropriate solutions quickly, literally passing over many of the architecture vision activities needed. Since the ADM is an iterative process, this may be acceptable to create the first transition architecture for the enterprise.
Third Best	A	The activities within this answer are valid and will essentially aid the architecture effort but there is no real context in place to understand the value of the activities: no vision is being developed nor any solution to be implemented.
Distracter	B	The project is a greenfield with essentially no architecture currently in place to assess. As a result, the remaining activities have no foundation of support.

15 References

The Open Group Architecture Framework Version 8.1.1, Enterprise Edition. The Open Group; April 2007.

The Open Group Architecture Framework Version 9. The Open Group; April 2009.

TOGAF information: www.openforum.org

Websites

www.artofservice.com.au
www.theartofservice.org
www.theartofservice.com

16 Index

A

B

baseline 15, 31, 34, 38, 42-4, 46-7, 49, 64, 93, 96, 109, 145-6, 153, 169
baseline architecture 28, 56-7, 64, 97, 109, 152-3, 159
business architecture 4-5, 15, 23, 34-5, 37-9, 41, 69, 145
business capability 14, 30, 74, 145, 165
business continuity requirements 68, 70-1
business goals 89, 154, 156-8, 170
business objectives 78, 80, 136, 149, 156-7, 160, 169
business principles 28, 30-4, 37, 80, 164
business processes 27, 36-7, 69, 89, 94, 96, 126, 145, 158
business scenarios 5-6, 33, 36, 62, 87-9, 105, 165

C

capabilities 14, 28, 32-3, 39, 47, 50, 58, 65, 81, 104, 119, 124, 144-5, 152, 155-7
Capability Maturity Models (CMMs) 4, 19, 29, 140
catalogs 6, 43, 101-2
CIO 152, 156, 158-9
commitment 26, 139, 156-7, 159, 170
completeness 38, 42-3, 46, 76, 101, 146
compliance 16, 18, 56, 80-1, 93, 104, 110, 134, 136, 140, 150
conflicts 38, 42-3, 46, 62, 69, 104, 120, 163, 169
continuum 116-17
costs 52, 69, 74, 82, 84, 90, 98, 142, 150, 155-8

D

data architecture 39-43, 102, 146
deliverables 106, 137, 153, 168, 170-1
design 1, 13, 21, 56, 73, 76, 81, 129, 144, 148, 154
developing 6, 21, 27, 33, 35, 37-8, 41-3, 46, 81, 105, 117, 137, 158, 173
diagrams 37, 41-2, 46, 101-4
drivers 5, 33, 58, 104, 156-7, 169

E

enterprise architects   13, 79, 154
Enterprise Continuum   3, 7, 16, 21, 116-17, 120-1, 144, 146, 148, 150-1, 166, 168
enterprise operations   38, 42-3, 46, 81
evaluation   138, 156
exam   1, 10-12

F

FEAF (Federal Enterprise Architecture Framework)   18, 80
Foundation Architecture   3, 21, 118, 146
framework   21, 23-4, 26-30, 53, 57, 60, 76, 79, 100, 113, 117, 138, 140, 146, 148, 163
functionality   82, 104, 114-15

G

gap analysis   6, 56, 60, 62, 91, 151, 153, 158, 167
goals   6, 29-35, 37, 41, 89, 99, 103-4, 112, 146-7, 150, 154-7, 164
governance framework   57, 99, 163, 172
guidance   17, 23, 57, 78, 89, 132-3, 138, 156, 159-60, 169

I

information systems   1, 50-1, 63, 126, 148, 155-8
infrastructure   58, 75, 81, 127-8, 148, 153-5, 160
inputs   29, 32, 40, 48-9, 52, 55, 59, 61, 69, 79, 85, 154-5, 158, 166
Intellectual Property   18, 82
interoperability   18, 24, 48, 74-6, 91, 94-5, 126-7, 146, 152, 155, 157
iterations   22, 25, 63-4, 66, 153

K

Key Performance Indicators (KPIs)   31, 33, 164
knowledge   10, 19, 35, 136, 141, 143, 146, 148

L

Lead Architect   150, 152-3, 162

M

matrix   6, 36, 41, 43, 92-3, 100-1, 150, 160-1
maturity models   6, 95, 97
Migration Plan   7, 51-3, 55, 59, 92, 95, 111, 151-3, 158-61, 171
models   19, 21, 25, 29-30, 36-7, 71, 87, 89, 97, 103, 116, 122, 147,
154-5, 159, 164

O

operations management   53, 58, 150

P

partitions   65, 122-3
policies   21, 47, 67, 70-1, 77, 79, 81-2, 84, 115, 145
portfolios   14, 47-8, 51, 55, 114
priorities   53, 56, 62
process models   118
processes, modeling   37, 41-2, 46

R

readiness   6, 85, 95, 97, 165
recommendations   54, 56-7, 60, 109, 156, 162, 172
reference models   11, 21, 120, 122, 129, 147
resources   17, 22, 25, 27, 30-1, 37, 40, 52-3, 59, 73, 78, 80, 85, 112,
147, 158
responsibilities   8, 14, 18, 26, 29, 81-3, 87-8, 111, 113, 132, 137-9,
160
RFC (Requests for Change)   58
risks   15, 25, 31, 33, 48, 50, 63, 69, 90, 95, 97-9, 142, 164, 167
roles   14, 19, 28-9, 88, 109, 111, 132, 136, 141-2, 148, 167

S

scenarios   36, 63, 88-9, 168
schedule   111, 113, 151, 159
scope   14-15, 24, 26-8, 31, 33, 35, 41, 52, 63-4, 104, 113, 136
security   20, 36, 68-9, 72-3, 83, 91, 104, 141, 152, 167
service levels   82, 103-4
skills   14, 19, 28, 56, 132, 142, 148
SOA (Service Oriented Architecture)   5, 74-7, 148, 154, 168
solutions phase   47-9, 51, 73
sponsors   31-2, 34, 89, 106, 137
stakeholder management   5, 14, 85, 145, 170

T

TOGAF (The Open Group Architecture Forum)   1, 3, 5, 7, 10-13, 15, 28, 61, 77, 85, 100, 117, 120, 128, 162, 168-9
Transition Architectures   4, 7, 48-9, 51-5, 65, 93, 111, 114, 149, 171, 173
TRM (Technical Reference Model)   7, 44, 93, 120, 126, 148

U

UML (Unified Modeling Language)   36
users   69, 72, 82-4, 106, 128, 138

V

value   1-2, 36, 69, 79, 82, 87, 119, 138-9, 173
vendors   10, 87, 115-16, 150-1

Breinigsville, PA USA
24 November 2009
228159BV00002B/57/P